*An Dun*

# THE CHINESE DREAM

Real-Life Stories of the Common People
in Contemporary China

新世界出版社
NEW WORLD PRESS

First Edition 2009

By An Dun
Translated by Li Yang, Zhang Ruiqing, and Pan Daqing
Illustrations by SOWO
Revised by Paul White
Edited by Li Shujuan and Ge Wencong
Cover Design by Qing Qing Chong Studio

ISBN 978-7-5104-0407-8

*Published by*
NEW WORLD PRESS
24 Baiwanzhuang Street, Beijing 100037, China

*Distributed by*
NEW WORLD PRESS
24 Baiwanzhuang Street, Beijing 100037, China
Tel: 86-10-68995968
Fax: 86-10-68998705
Website: www. newworld-press. com
E-mail: frank@ nwp. com. cn

*Printed in the People's Republic of China*

# Contents

# Foreword

Every nation has its own dream. From the middle of the 19th century imperialist countries rode roughshod over China. The dream of public-spirited Chinese at the end of the Qing Dynasty (1644—1911) was to make China an independent nation which could hold its own in the world. After overthrowing the Qing Empire, the Chinese dreamed of removing the "three big mountains" of imperialism, feudalism and bureaucrat-capitalism, and establishing a new China. Today in socialist China our dream is to achieve the goal of an all-round well-off society step by step by the 100th anniversary of the People's Republic of China in 2049. A nation without a dream is a tragic one, for without goals there can be no challenges. A nation's dream has to be the dream of all her children; otherwise it must be like "a castle in the air," which can not be realized. The success of the Chinese revolution lies in the fact that the basis of the nation's dream was the dream of its people.

In recent years I have participated several times in the "Forum on the Dream of the Chinese and the Building of a Harmonious Society" held by Wu Jianmin, president of the China Foreign Affairs University and former ambassador to France. Most of the participants are those who have been successful in this new era of reform and innovation, and their dreams are all closely related to the dream of the nation itself. The forum found a basis for our nation's dream: the dream of the "elites." But what are the dreams of the common people? The answer lies at a deeper level. To our joy, the author of this book has filled this gap that couldn't be ignored by interviewing ordinary young Chinese people who are not "elites" but still cherish their own dreams that may represent the wishes of the majority of the Chinese people.

These ordinary people struggled to realize their dreams, experiencing success and failure, learned lessons and sometimes felt regret. The true and touching stories are presented without embellishment, in their original form. None of these young people gave up. Their dreams pushed forward both themselves and their society. I hope they will always be confident and courageous. Their dreams are part of the nation's dream, and they are just like thousands of "Changzheng carrier rockets" soaring aloft with China's dreams. With such strong engines, China's dream will certainly fly directly to the day it becomes true.

In March 2006, several friends and I were introduced by Zhang Hai'ou, Deputy Editor-in-Chief of the New World Press, to An Dun, to talk about publishing some books of mine. Starting with the "dialogues" of my *Tell the World about China*, we discussed sincerity in communication, how to communicate with others, and the relationship between self-confidence and being bold and assured because of the righteousness of one's cause. But An Dun said, "I'm not going to ask anything about your distinguished past. Let's just talk about your daily life." Then she expressed her interest in knowing about my friends. So, pointing at Zhou Mingwei, a learned scholar and Executive Deputy President of the China International Publishing Group, who happened to be there, I said that he was one of my best friends. Then she asked him, point-blank: "Tell me about Zhao Qizheng's shortcomings." At the end, she told us that she had been interviewing us.

Before long, her "oral record" was published. My elderly mother, a retired professor, after reading it through, commented, "I could guess that it's none other than Qizheng, even if your name was not mentioned. It's simple, sincere, and excellent!" An Dun's "oral record" shows her great originality. She is good at introducing a topic and summing up its essence. She has a subtle approach to both her interviewees and readers. All in all, her work is truly unique.

This book highlights the uniqueness of her style: You understand something great from something seemingly trivial. When I read these true, moving stories, I felt as if I were joining in their talk, and was delighted to make 13 precious new friends whom a man of my age would normally never meet and befriend at all.

I believe the readers will share my feelings.

Zhao Qizheng

Note: Zhao Qizheng, former Director-General of the State-Council Information Office, Director of the Committee of Foreign Affairs of the Chinese People's Political Consultative Conference, and Dean of the School of Journalism and Communication of Renmin University of China.

# To Hold Your Hand,
# To Grow Old with You

**Time of interview**: January 2003 till 2008

**Place**: Starbucks Coffee, Beijing Sunflower Tower

Starbucks Coffee, Beijing World Trade Center

Qu Shan, female, 49, majored in the Chinese language at university. Qu was once a teacher at a university in Beijing, and moved to New Zealand with her husband in 1999. Qu is now running a school in Wellington to promote Chinese culture and the Chinese language.

**I think that the person who had the greatest influence on me was my Chinese-language teacher in middle school. He was once the most perfect person in my life, and that of a teacher, I thought, was the most perfect career.**

I always remember the way you looked when attending my classes at the university. I was teaching the poems of Su Dongpo on that day, and I caught your eyes when reading the following lines: "Ten years, dead and living dim and drawing apart. I don't try to remember, but forgetting is hard." I didn't know why, and I was wondering if I could put an end to my long love story and tell it to someone someday, I would tell it to you. I knew that you would be grown up when I did this.

I was wondering whether you could understand the influence one person has on another. If you love someone, you will be fascinated by his career, temperament, culture and style, and so on. You will be eager to know more about such a nice personality, and will also get close to his style and the way he lives, unconsciously, which will then become an influence on you as time goes by. It will affect your choices in your relationships, career, and direction. It will gradually become a kind of inertia. You will become more and more like him. Finally, you will find that you've already lived a life similar to his for a long time.

Suddenly, I don't know how to make it clear, but I know you can understand. Just like a story, or a book you're obsessed with, you want to be one of the characters in it. You are easily influenced when you are young. It happens to girls roughly at puppy love time. The influence one person has on another is so powerful that it may even go beyond your imagination.

I'd better start from my own experience, or it will be a bit confusing. I just want to say that I think the person who influenced me most was my Chinese-language teacher in middle school. For me, he was once the most perfect person in my life, and I decided to become a teacher too.

I remember the day I got married. My friends joined in the fun, and said that my husband was a lucky man, as he had married a woman who had never fallen in love before. One of my female colleagues held me in her arms, and said that if I hadn't got married they would have taken me to a hospital to find out what was wrong with me. Actually, I had not had any relationship before, yet I loved someone secretly. He was older than I—my Chinese-language teacher in middle school. He was old enough to be my father. I came back in 2003, when he had passed away. His wife had wanted me to see him before he died. I so regretted only seeing him after he died.

I would like to say that the memory of my intense stare at my teacher has accompanied me throughout my life. I looked at him sleeping quietly. I'd never stared at him in such way. Even during the time he was gentle and handsome, or the period I admired and was crazy about him, I'd never gazed at him in that way, and he also didn't give me an opportunity to see him in that way. He was dynamic in my eyes before I gazed at him, though he had always been calm and quiet. I dared not stare at him, and I'd never looked at him in such an unveiled way, so painful, full of natural feeling. Only one thought floated into my mind then, that was, he left me, he left me forever. Let me just take a good look at him! He used to be the last person I would let go of in the memory of my youth, and I can only meet him in dreams in the following years!

Instead of crying over his remains, I was calm in my heart. I held his hands, brushed his sleeves, and confirmed that the time on his watch was right... I did not break down when doing these things, yet my whole body was trembling, as if there were a needle pricking me right to my heart. My teacher's wife stood on one side, held my other hand, and said, "Dear, don't be like that. You just cry, cry out loud, and he will hear you."

He could not hear me, and he did not know I had ever cried for him. For so many years, he and his wife only saw my smiling face. Just like a dutiful child, I tried hard to convey happiness at least.

I'm particularly excited, right? I dare not say what happened at that time, nor can I describe what I felt. I just felt that my heart was broken. My teacher's wife was a thin old lady. She held me in her arms, and I could feel that she was trembling. My teacher took away my care for him for half of my life, and also took away the last hope of his wife.

I don't want to recall that painful experience. Using a metaphor you use in your novels, that was a kind of burning in the heart.

I think I was very lucky, as I met a good man, a wonderful teacher, and an amazing husband—of course, a good husband for his wife, and a fantastic father for me—he had a greater meaning for me than my real father.

What I'm going to tell you is actually a story about secret love. I can't remember where I saw the lines saying that secret love is the most humble feeling in the world. In fact, this is not the case. The one who said that must not have been involved in a true secret love, as she only saw one side of herself, yet not the happiness when one loves another after forgetting her own existence. I have always been very happy since the first day I felt that he occupied all my heart. I still get such a feeling.

It is common for girl students to like their teachers in novels and movies.

Most of the stories end in sadness. In contrast, I think I was very lucky, as I met a good man, a wonderful teacher, and an amazing husband—of course, a good husband for his wife, and a fantastic father for me—he had a greater meaning for me than my real father.

I finally chose to learn Chinese due to his influence. He got me interested in the Chinese language in a very short time. Chinese is such a rich, exquisite and delicate language, particularly subtle and restrained. The first lesson he taught was *The Battle of the Red Cliff*. I can not figure out what happened to him on that day, as he was supposed to teach from the textbook, or at least introduce other famous battles, but he spent most of the time talking about the *Ode to the Goddess of the Luo River*. Even today, I still feel that this came from the mind of a man falling in love with someone secretly. I can recite the entire text.

Many people describe their first lover as cool and handsome. I never say that, as it was not the case. My teacher was already a middle-aged man the first time I met him, just like an old man, in fact. I prefer to say that he was special, gentle and calm, with purity in his eyes. I feel that it was a kind of cultivation after reading books for years. I still remember what I thought at that time: How amazing it would be if he were a part of my family!

I also became a teacher many years later. I always look in the mirror at home, and recite what I am going to say before I enter the classroom every day. I examine my image, intonation and expression. I begin to miss him at that moment. I hope the way I stand on the podium can be similar to his. He always looked totally calm, wise and collected. Even though my students can speak little Chinese, I still keep this habit. I have a deep-rooted belief that teachers are always role models for their pupils. My experience teaches me that teachers have a civilizing influence on students.

According to my students, I am a wise and elegant teacher, and a delicate and gentle lady. Girls should be like that after they grow up. I am extremely proud of their opinion of me. Besides, I think that no one knows how I became such a woman. How did I perfect myself? I was the very person who knew the reason: My teacher always offered me guidelines and instruction during this self-improvement process.

Back to the story.

My best friend then was the monitor of our class. Both of her parents were teachers at the school, and she lived in the staff building with her family. You know, girls always do things for their own interests. I wanted to get closer to my teacher through my best friend. I always did my homework at her house. The door used to be open, and only a curtain separated her apartment from the corridor leading to the apartment where my teacher lived. I could hear his footsteps after work, and sometimes could even see his legs as he walked past the curtain. No matter how many people passed, I knew exactly which legs were his. I used to pack my bag and go home for dinner after I saw him pass. I felt very satisfied that the day had not been wasted.

I learned something about his family from the monitor. He didn't have any children, and his wife used to be a worker in the school-run factory. He came from a village in Jiangsu Province, and the marriage had been arranged. His wife was illiterate. When I heard this I could not quite understand why such a cultured man could marry a peasant woman? Could they share a common language? Could she read his mind? I felt sorry for him. He must have been depressed having to maintain the marriage for fear he would be criticized and laughed at by others if he abandoned his wife.

I liked to attend his classes, and prepared the lessons well every day. I also collected materials related to the text. I hoped I would be asked to answer questions, so that I could stand up and talk to him face to face. I was tall in senior high school. When I stood up to answer questions, my eyes could meet his easily, which made me feel that we were separated by no distance. Silly, right? Women are always silly when they fall in love. They will even relish every detail thousands of times, or even tens of thousands of times.

I sensed that he liked me. For him, that was rather a teacher's love and appreciation for his student. Yet for me, I preferred to believe that there was an additional ambiguous feeling between a man and a woman. It would be hard for me to cherish him in my mind for a whole 25 years without such a firm belief.

I was eventually chosen to be the representative of the Chinese-language

class, thanks to my diligence. There is probably no lower "official" than a representative in a middle school, yet it was my dream at that time. I finally got the chance to do things for him—I had to collect the homework, compositions and test papers of my classmates, and then deliver them to him. I thereby had an excuse to go to his office. Besides, I had to go to his office again and collect all these materials once he had checked them. So I had more reasons to get close to him than other students had. It was so fantastic! I am not good at writing, though I've been teaching Chinese all these years, yet for the last year at senior high school, I brainstormed to write every composition just to win his appreciation. I've never written a love letter in my life, but I wrote every composition as a love letter to him at that time. I collected every book checked and corrected by him. The reviews he wrote in red ink have faded, yet I can still feel the heartbeat and blushing I experienced every time I looked at those words. We exchanged letters for many years, and none of these could surpass the reviews he wrote for me at that time.

I had to take the college entrance examination in the final year of senior high school. You know, during the time shortly after the resumption of the entrance examination, people of my generation spent little time studying, as we had no confidence. I was invited to his home during the most tense period. I still remember that it happened before we left school. At that time he offered us the last Chinese lesson. Then he came straight to my desk, stooped low, and said, "Will you come to my home for dinner tonight? I would like to talk to you about the upcoming exam." I was too nervous and excited to say anything. I simply nodded my head. He said that he would write down his address for me. I blurted out "It's not necessary. I know where you live." I shocked myself saying this. It was equivalent to telling him my closest secret, wasn't it? He smiled gently.

His apartment was small, only two rooms. It was hard for a poor teacher to get a good apartment at that time. One room was used as a study and as a living room; the other was the bedroom. Nevertheless, his wife kept the place spotless, inside and outside, with everything well organized. My teacher's wife was thin and nice, and looked older than she actually was. Probably, women were not rich enough to dress themselves up during that period. That was the first time I saw her. At that time, I got the impression that she could not be classified as peasant woman. I didn't know what kind of education she had received. Actually, she was definitely not an unlearned or ungracious person. Instead, her bearing could help her win the respect of anyone.

My teacher's wife was not talkative, and what she cooked was rather delicious. They were typical southern dishes, light and delicate. She ate quickly, and retired to the bedroom, saying, "You two enjoy yourselves." For so many years, my teacher's wife was always a virtuous and kind-hearted woman as far as I was concerned. Besides, the last time I went to see them before I got married, I realized that she might be the one who knew me best. She knew from the very beginning that I had fallen in love with her husband, though I didn't think anyone else realized. She gave me a jade bracelet wrapped in red silk on that day, and said, "My dear, you are finally getting married. This is part of the betrothal gift I received when I married your teacher. I give one bracelet to you, and I will keep the other. That one will also go to you after I pass away. We have no children, so I have regarded you as my own child for many years." She never said what she had learned or guessed. Women are always the best mind-readers of other women, sometimes, even without any explanation.

It was literally on that day that I decided to choose the Chinese language as my major. And I also wanted to be a teacher, a teacher like him. I told him about what I thought, and he was so surprised that he stared at me for a long time. Then he asked me why. I replied, "For no reason, I just like it, and I don't think there is any career more attractive than that of a teacher, as I can find what I want there." He nodded with a smile, and said meaningfully: "Anyway, I hope you won't regret it." I said, "I'm sure I won't."

I went to my teacher's home frequently after that, just like I had got some kind of permission. He also welcomed my visits, and I could feel that he was eager for my success, specifically, to have my university dream fulfilled.

Everything went smoothly for me. It was a miracle for me to be enrolled by a university, due to my poor academic performance at that time. I prefer to believe that it was the power of love that drove me to study hard in the final stage, even forgetting food and sleep.

**My father's generation should not be classified as people who didn't know how to love. In fact, the simplicity contained in their love can embarrass the young who frequently talk about love nowadays.**

I should be counted as a brave person among girls at that time, as I chose to speak my feelings out, regardless of what might happen. On the occasion of the first Spring Festival after I entered the college, many of my classmates agreed to visit our teacher, and we went to his home. They left one after another after a happy hour. I was the last one to leave, and he insisted on seeing me off. We passed through the small playground and went for a ramble on a path to the school gate. He told me repeatedly to take care of myself, and I suddenly felt very sentimental, especially when I saw his silver hair flashing under the light during the dinner. He was old, the man I loved was already getting old, but I hadn't grown up yet. I took his arm, and said that I had something to tell him, and I could only talk to him after we had stopped walking. He didn't push my hand away. He stopped walking, and said "All right." His smile seemed so gentle under the street lamp that I could not be calm, and I didn't know how to start. He was standing in front of me, waiting for me. I didn't know how long it would be, all I knew was that he smiled and remained in the same position. I finally began to speak. I told him that I had worked hard to study Chinese because of him, I had chosen the teaching profession as my life-long career because of him, and I had striven to find reasons to do my homework at the monitor's home just to see his legs walking by.... I can't remember what else I said at that time.

He listened to me silently till I stopped and stared at him. Then he pulled his arm away, raised it slowly, and touched my hair. He stroked my hair tenderly. I had no idea what he would say or how he would judge me after I had told him what was on my mind. All I could do was wait. The waiting then seemed longer than the whole of the past 25 years.

He said, "My dear girl, I know. "

His voice was particularly calm, no emotional fluctuation, no worry about being loved by a student. Nothing else, just these simple words.

I didn't know how long it was before he asked me: "Do you want to know what had happened between my wife and me?"

I nodded, feeling like my soul was hooked by something, and then began waiting.

He took my hand, and we walked toward a street lamp. He asked me to sit on the roadside. He then began to tell me an older story than what I told you today.

He and his wife grew up together in the same village. They were good friends in childhood. His mother died early. He was the eldest son of the family, followed by two younger brothers. Their father was the breadwinner for the whole family. The mother of my teacher's wife was very kind and honest. She could not bear to see that no one repaired the worn clothes or prepared hot meals for the four men. She even made a decision that shocked the whole village. She asked her daughter to be the mistress of my teacher's family to take care of their lives without a wedding ceremony. My teacher's wife was younger than 16 then, and was a bride in all but name in the village. His family was poor, only a pair of jade bracelets left by his mother was given to the bride as a betrothal gift. Later he got an opportunity to go to a teacher-training school in the town without paying any tuition fees. Despite that, the family became poorer than before. My teacher's wife and the whole family tried hard to support the "scholar" who had left the village. Then he got the opportunity to go to Beijing and become a teacher in a middle school.

After he went to Beijing, his wife remained with her father-in-law and two brother-in-laws, taking care of their lives. She even planned to send his brothers to school and was concerned about their marriage. My teacher and his wife actually lived separate lives.

I got to know why they had no children that day. My teacher's wife was pregnant after his return to the village the first time. Unfortunately, she had a miscarriage after five months. She was still working at a small factory in the village at that time. She nearly died, and could not have any more babies.

When I look back now I feel that the day he told me what he and his wife experienced was the most unforgettable day of my life. I think I was still too young to understand responsibility, gratitude and mutual dependence, and selfless love. But I figured out one thing that even though I had such a strong crush on him, it was insignificant compared to what his wife had done for him.

What else could I say? All my words were overwhelmed by this story. I have always been moved when I thought of them, my teacher and his wife, over the years. The older I get, the more real the feeling is. My father's generation should not be classified as people who don't know how to love. In fact, the simplicity contained in their love can embarrass the young who frequently talk about love nowadays, just like myself at that time.

I told my students the story of my teacher. I said that the story would evolve to another ending nowadays. For instance, the man went to the town and then went abroad. He finished his study with the woman's hard-earned money, or under the woman's intense care. Finally, after the man became somebody, the so-called cultural differences split the couple. Then a refined and civilized woman appeared, outshone the ordinary wife, and became an excellent match for the man. Finally, cultural differences became a perfect excuse for a breakup. If the man was conscientious, he might compensate the woman financially. If not, the woman would just be abandoned. Such stories happen frequently. Don't these men ever think that before they discovered the so-called differences, they actually helped to create these cultural gaps? With this consideration, I was moved by the story of my teacher as it contained both love and morality.

**I think I was lucky and blessed to get to know such a good family and such an amazing couple.**

It is fair to say that my life later was related to that person in some way. Perhaps, he is my ideal love. He became a criterion, and I always try to find the other part of my life, modeled on him. Or I can say he had nothing to do with me, as he didn't show up when I was waiting for the man who deserved to be loved by me. Finally, my husband came into my life.

I didn't tell him about my feelings any more after that night. Deep in my heart, he was my teacher, my father and a friend I admired. I often went to see him and his wife, taking them fresh fruit and vegetables every time. I could remember when his gas bottle needed changing. I also helped my teacher's wife to unpick and wash the cotton quilts for winter.... She weaved me a thick sweater with nice wool.... I became like their daughter for many years after that night.

I think I was lucky and blessed to get to know such a good family and such an amazing couple. I saw them aging gradually. After his retirement, my teacher always held his wife's hand when they went out to buy vegetables and walked around in the morning. My teacher read a book by the window while his wife was choosing fresh vegetables or sewing, wearing a pair of glasses. I felt particularly warmed by these scenes.

I once wrote a letter to my teacher, and asked him: Do you love your wife? I didn't mean love with responsibility, but a man's pure love for a woman who loves and understands him. He wrote back and said: "A woman can risk her own life for you, give up once-in-a-lifetime opportunity to ask for a grand wedding ceremony, accompany you quietly without any compliment, whether life is good or tough. She won't leave you when you are in bad times. She won't dislike and avoid you when you are old and sick. She requires no return but to keep each other company for life. If you were a man, would you love such a woman?"

I showed this letter to my husband, and he said, "Qu Shan, maybe our kids will not be able to understand such a relationship in the future, but I still feel that we will always be moved." I think what my husband said is actually what I want to say.

I went to accompany my teacher's wife on the night of "the seventh day" [according to Chinese funeral customs, on the seventh day the deceased's ghost comes back home. So on that day the family will prepare his favorite food or things for his return to express their last regards.] for my teacher. She was almost 80 years old. I was the only "member of the family" for her after my teacher passed away.

My teacher's wife called, and told me that my teacher was about to die. She said, "Visit him if you can come back home." It was such a simple sentence that drove my husband and me to go back, leaving aside all work and our children. But as soon as we got to the hospital he had already died. He had a calm expression. While looking at him, I felt as if I had gone back to senior high school. For the first time I saw him, he was teaching us the *Battle of the Red Cliff* and the *Ode to the Goddess of the Luo River*. I still feel that I love this man with a love different from my feeling towards any other person in the world. Here I would like to thank my husband. He knows this 25-year story, and he hasn't deprived me of the right to keep this love deep in my heart. He said that he respected my teacher as well, and was proud of the other "family" I had.

My teacher's wife gave the other jade bracelet to me on the day my teacher was cremated. The bracelet was still wrapped in red silk. She opened the silk, took the bracelet and put it on me with her own shaking hands. She said, "My girl, if there is an afterlife, I would rather we were still a family." What she said actually helped remove the shame deep in my heart. I think I should be regarded as a noble person, right? After all, I did not intervene in their relationship when I began to suspect their marriage was shaky, and I was touched by the nobility of the pair. I was still a person who could admire and support a wonderful relationship.

My teacher's wife died in April 2008. For the six days from her sickness to her death, I was always by her side. After the death of my teacher, my husband and I both asked her to go abroad and live together with us, so we could take good care of her and let her leave the environment where she and my teacher lived together. My teacher was the only and whole center of her life. Her feeling towards my teacher was far more than a simple love. She only promised to tell me any problem or difficulty in her life through a regular phone conversation. But she said she couldn't leave the house. She said, "Dear, he has gone and you've gone abroad, I'm the only person at home. If I don't look after the house, what will you do if you come back? I will just look after the house for you. Go anywhere you want, just don't forget to come back. "

I hired a nanny for her when I left Beijing, and asked my younger brother to visit her regularly. I also gave her at least one phone call every week, and treated her like my mother. Due to my feeling towards my teacher, I felt a stronger responsibility to look after her after his death.

She was very calm at the final moment. She said, "Dear, I'm going to join him. Do you have anything for me to tell him?" I could say nothing. I was almost 50, and I had a daughter. I also began to face my daughter's puppy love thing, yet at this moment, I returned to the past. Just like a child immersed in puppy love, I had lots to say, yet didn't know how to start.

She placed her hand on my head, gently. She said, "Dear, I know what you are going to say. If there is an afterlife, we will meet each other again. . . . "

I was the executor of her will. My teacher led a rather poor life, with no property to leave. His widow entrusted me to sell the house and send the money to the two brothers of my teacher. This money can secure them a comfortable life in their old age. After the funeral expenses were deducted, the couple had less than 20,000 yuan in the bank. They wanted to give this money to the nanny who had taken care of them. My teacher's books and souvenirs were left to me. My teacher's wife organized things well in her final days. Obviously, she had thought these things over.

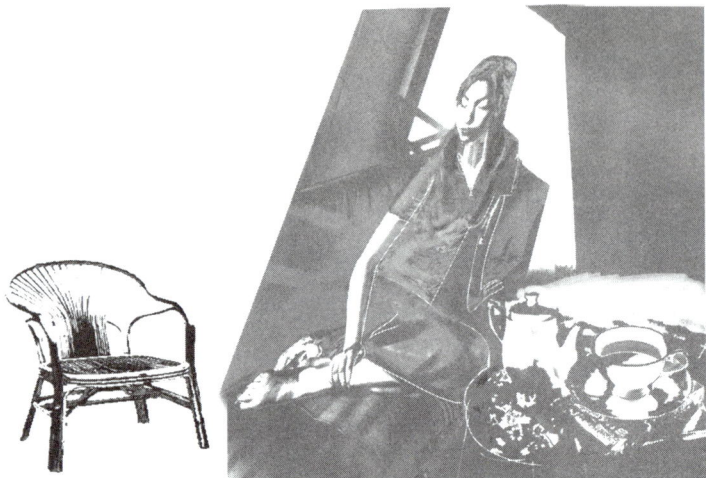

On the day of the house ownership transfer, I sat in the place I had often sat, with my teacher's sofa on one side, and his wife's cane chair on the other side. There was tea on the table and the latest newspaper at hand. I felt as if the whole family were chatting together. My teacher burst out laughing from time to time at what I said, and his wife looked at us over her glasses, with a smile on her face. . . .

If there is afterlife, we will meet each other again.

## Interviewer's Notes

### Missing Classical Love

I studied economics in college. I was not a good student, as I didn't like my major. I often snatched a little leisure from a busy life to attend a classical literature course at a university nearby. It was roughly at that period that I met Qu Shan. I called her "Miss Qu. " She was very beautiful back then, not such a typical beauty, yet very special. I learned a word specially applied to women—femininity. The first thought that struck me was that the word was really made for her.

We were not only teacher and student, but also cross-generation friends. Qu Shan was still single then. She was already 37 years old when she got married. Her husband had a Ph. D in Architecture, engaging in large-scale urban architectural design. It was said that she had no relationships before her marriage. I became a reporter when she got married. When I asked about her relationships, she said, "Simple and complex. It's a long story. I will tell you when the time is right."

Miss Qu went back to Beijing and called me in early 2003. I asked the purpose of her trip, and she said, "Not a visit to relatives or friends, just a funeral." I thought that might be the "right time."

We met at the coffee bar in the office building opposite to the Landmark Flower Market. She wore a black coat, black sweater, black shirt, black trousers, and black boots, and carried a black leather bag. A white necklace formed the only color contrast. She chose the place, and said she wanted to buy 25 lilies for a person she had cared for over 25 years.

I wrote down the following lines in my interview notes: "I don't know whether the glass window of the cafe was light blue. Talking about a past event with a woman who has gone through half her life's journey, I actually feel that the small piece of sky outside the window is gradually turning into eye-catching blue, and becoming imperceptibly wider. Many nice people and beautiful things in the world cannot be possessed by us, yet a person pursuing beauty will still choose to be with them silently—with never any separation." Qu Shan told me a very long story, and the details of her "humble secret love" would occupy far more than that. I took too long writing this story, as I was not sure whether people would be moved by these two classical relationships nowadays.

It happened to be Valentine's Day when I wrote this story. The streets were full of romance, and roses and chocolates were sold at sky-high prices. Who would care about these people with no roses or chocolates in their relationships, or no romantic sentence like "to hold your hand and grow old with you"? Yet they have always been "holding hands" and "growing old" with the one they loved all their lives.

I called Qu Shan on the evening of Valentine's Day, and asked what else she would like to say. She finally decided to write to me after a long time of thinking about it.

I found the ending written by Qu Shan after "racking her brains" on the QQ message board:

"That was a classical love. In these fashionable times, when new emerging things are doomed to be eliminated as soon as they appear, I miss classical love, as it is a splendid performance which would never drop the curtain deep in my soul.

"I am now a mother of two, and the wife of a dedicated and family man. I gradually learned the simple truth about happiness when I was occupied in bread-and-butter issues. For lovers, it is their ideal to keep each other company for life. It needs time, patience, wisdom, tolerance, dedication and responsibility all one's life.

"I think I've found the right person, be it in the past or now. After you find the right one, make the most of every single day with him. Life is literally composed of these single days."

When we parted, Qu Shan told me that our next conversation must be connected with a funeral. I knew she was referring to the funeral of her teacher's wife.

Five years passed.

Qu Shan came back to China several times to see her teacher's wife. Instead of living in her mother's house or a hotel, she always lived with her teacher's wife. She said there wasn't much time left for her teacher's wife. When a woman particularly cares about a man, she won't keep him waiting for long. Qu always choked with sobs when saying such things, and our conversation also stopped then.

I went to visit Qu Shan when she was taking care of the funeral affairs for her teacher's wife. I saw a family portrait of the three. The old couple sat quietly in the front row while Qu Shan stood behind, draping her arms around them.

I used to describe the story of Qu Shan in the following words, "To hold your hand and to grow old with you." When I saw this picture, I felt that the words were still applicable. The only difference was that there were three people holding hands together. Parents and a daughter, a couple and a woman, a teacher and a student, and two women and one man. . . . These simple and complex relationships were greatly simplified by them, simplified to the most beautiful things ever, sparking golden-like lights during the long years. You can definitely see it if you have a heart of gold.

# *It Seems I Am Still*
# *at the Earthquake Site*

**Time of interview:** May 27, 29, 2008

Cui Jun, male, 41, photojournalist of *Beijing Youth Daily*

Zhang Hongjiang, male, 41, journalist of the *Beijing Evening News*

**Cui Jun: It was the most memorable experience of my journalistic career so far, but I would rather this disaster hadn't occurred.**

I've been back for days. I haven't reviewed the photos in the computer. I wouldn't have looked at them if you hadn't asked me to recount my days there by showing each of them. I'm not afraid to look at them. If I were afraid, I wouldn't have taken them. Really, I'm not afraid. The reason why I don't want to review them is that I'm not willing to. Yes, I'm not willing to, but I'm not afraid. If you ask other photojournalists who were at the disaster area, they would probably say the same. All those things are in my brain, like a movie displayed there, and I can see it without closing my eyes. I can recall those loud noises I had never heard before, which even Hollywood movies can't imitate, including the noises of the falling sky and the cracking earth, and people crying for help, calling to each other and howling. Those noises are all mixed up and impossible to bear. After I came back, I got many invitations to "welcome-back dinners" or "calm-your-nerve dinners." I just sat among the other people, drinking. Sometimes I went distracted while drinking, and my mind went back to those days when I had nothing to eat or drink. I just thought: I'm back alive. It's so wonderful!

And then there would be so many buts. But so many died just in a minute without any preparation or notice. They were living their lives step by step. Some were studying at school, some were working, and some were preparing their wedding ceremonies. Some women were about to give birth, and some old men were taking a nap at the time. Suddenly everything changed dramatically. At the thought of this I feel very ridiculous. Really, when we were young we all shouted the slogan that man can conquer nature, but before a sudden disaster, how tiny and passive man is! Can we really conquer nature? I ask this question maybe because I suddenly understand there are really some gloomy moments in life. As a result, we need a power that gives us reasons to survive optimistically in those gloomy moments. Back from the disaster area, I feel lucky. Many people like me are very lucky. We are lucky because we are alive, healthy and safe, and besides, we have chances and lots of time to do the things we like and look for our lovers. How luxurious this is!

Before arriving in the disaster area, I had no idea about it at all. I was in Lhasa on May 12, and had just finished interviews about the Olympic Torch Relay to Mount Qomolangma (Everest). Together with Zhang Hongjiang from the *Beijing Evening News*, I flew to Chengdu, capital of Sichuan Province, and then went directly to Dujiangyan by taxi. The 56-year-old taxi driver refused to accept the taxi fare when he heard we were from Beijing and that we were going to the disaster area for interviews. Dujiangyan was as far as the driver could go in the direction of Wenchuan, the disaster area, as the road was ruined. Zhang Hongjiang and I agreed that we must go to the epicenter for investigation. Don't ask whether I wanted to be a hero by doing that, for we didn't expect that we could be the first journalists to be there at all. After so many years of journalistic experience, it had become an instinct to go wherever an emergency had taken place. After making the decision, we had to minimize our luggage, for it was said to be 40 kilometers from there to the county town of Wenchuan. We left the stuff we didn't need with the taxi driver, and bought some bottles of water, instant noodles, a bag of salt and a bottle of liquor from a tiny store which had survived the earthquake. I have some survival experience. I know that salt is important. It saves one from dehydration. Liquor helps you resist the cold, and sterilizes. It was cold there and often rained in those days. Usually when I was woken up by cold at midnight I would take a big mouthful of the liquor so that I could warm up.

Dujiangyan was in a mess, with many houses ruined by the earthquake. Our journey to Yingxiu Town, the epicenter, started from there, and our direction was opposite to that of the refugees.

Huang, the taxi driver, left his mobile phone number with us. He didn't tell us he was worried about us, but later on I understood that he doubted whether we would come back alive. So when we were back in Chengdu and called him on May 18, he hurried over with our stuff, as well as fruit and cigarettes. He said that when he had had no news of us on the 16th, he had the local radio station make an announcement. But it was impossible to find us. At the time he really thought we would never come back.

Zhang Hongjiang was lucky. He was very cool. It is typical of artists that their brains are slower than other people's, so they don't fear anything. He said he wasn't afraid, but I didn't think he was telling the truth. How couldn't he be afraid? The first night was the most frightening for both us and the refugees, as there was no public information. Hearing worrying rumors from people coming out of the epicenter and experiencing constant aftershocks, we felt as if the sky were falling and the earth in upheaval.

We met some people fleeing, some injured. They urged us not to go there, but the more they tried to persuade us, the more eager we were to go. Among them was a person from Hangzhou who had gone to look for his wife and daughter on a visit to relatives in Yingxiu when the earthquake struck. He didn't know whether they were alive or not, but was determined to find them. A young guy from Zigong had been there working, with some others from his hometown. He was right outside Yingxiu when the disaster happened. He wanted to go and check whether his friends were safe. So a small group of us drove in together. We were stopped by a cliff edge. Aftershocks were violent and big rocks were falling off the mountainsides. The road became increasingly narrower, with mountains on one side and a river on the other.

Zhang Hongjiang urged me to drive throughout the night, but I didn't agree. Our head lights couldn't reach far; the rain was heavy; big rocks were falling off the mountain occasionally; and everything was collapsing in the near distance. "No, we mustn't go at night," I said, "we might be hit by a falling rock." Our companions were afraid, too, and so we stopped.

We were lucky to find an abandoned tourist bus parked in the road some 20 meters from the foot of the mountain, safe from falling rocks. We climbed into the bus through a broken window, and spent the night inside. The others would jump out whenever they heard a loud noise, but Zhang Hongjiang and I stayed inside, for even if we jumped off there would be nowhere to hide. It was a long night. We had the feeling of waiting for death, and were extremely nervous.

We continued our journey in the morning. After that night, strangely, we were no longer very afraid. At the time we hadn't seen the earthquake site, so we didn't know how destructive the disaster had been.

On the morning of the 14th we arrived in Yingxiu. It was impossible to go any further because the road to Wenchuan had been destroyed. We didn't know that Yingxiu was the epicenter until the 16th. Full-scale rescue activities hadn't begun when we arrived there, and the picture we saw was horrifying, with corpses lying all over the place.

I became a "thief" in the disaster area. I had to. When we abandoned the bus I took away its seat covers, a shabby overcoat and an old jacket. I reckoned that they would be useful. Old clothes can keep you as warm as new ones, and the seat covers could serve as bandages. Later on, as our food gave out, we searched everywhere for food like beggars. Zhang Hongjiang got water from a spring. Our companions, who knew the area, dug out food from the ruins of houses. This way we got bottles of beer and some potatoes, as well as a half-bottle of oil. We boiled those potatoes. They tasted good. Later, when a newspaper reported that I had died, a survivor said he had seen me boiling potatoes.

Then our work began. I don't know how to tell you about something that occurred afterwards. It is too depressing. Though it's my job and I'm a man, and I know the responsibility of a photojournalist isn't to cry but to record what he sees and show it to more people to let them come to help people there, still I couldn't control my emotion. Life is so vulnerable. There were dead bodies right beside our temporary shelter. When I was photographing a small school, I saw a fallen wall, and children beside the wall. ... You can't imagine and don't ever imagine. That would make you very sad. I saw everything in person, and I am sad. "When a photojournalist is at work, he is not allowed to weep, for tears will make him lose the focus. I must control myself. " I often said that to myself later on.

During my interviews, several times I was very emotional. Zhang Hongjiang called me crazy, which probably meant I couldn't control myself.

One time was body identification. When the earthquake occurred children were having classes, so most of them didn't survive. Some of them couldn't be identified. Their bodies were laid out in a row waiting for their parents to claim them. Some parents could spot their children straightaway, but others couldn't. Some parents lost their lives in the disaster, and some got injured. I'm sitting here now, but I can recall that scene. Their beloved children died in a flash, and they had to identify their bodies from the body pile, pick them up and incinerate or bury them together with all their hope and love for their children. I couldn't take pictures of them. That was the first time I had that feeling. I held the camera, but it was too hard for me to take a picture. Several times I got to the scene, but every time I left without taking a picture, as if I had gone mad. I just felt annoyed and depressed. Not until press time that afternoon did I take a few pictures, and leave in a hurry. I really couldn't stand it. At the time I felt that I was a human being first and a journalist second. Many journalists like Frank Capa's famous saying—If your pictures are not good enough, you are not close enough. That day, however, I knew I was close enough, but I couldn't conquer human emotion.

Another time I was taking the picture of Jiang Yuhang, who had just been rescued. It was like magic. His mother came from Guizhou Province just to check whether he was still alive, and I was at the scene then. Someone told her: "That's him, the one being dug out." The rescue process lasted about 80 hours. His mother stayed there from the beginning to the end, calling his name. At last the boy was rescued. I took many pictures of them. Later on I thought there must be some secret passage connecting parents and their children.

During those days in Yingxiu you could often see special message boards. They were just scraps of paper with such words as "xxx, we have gone to xxx. If you see this message, come and find us." They were hung on trees or broken walls. Some people, learning we were leaving for Chengdu, asked us to take messages to their families, saying that they were safe, while they remained behind to help the survivors.

Another very touching thing was the flag flown half-mast. As far as I could remember, it was the first time the Chinese government had ever arranged a three-day mourning period for ordinary victims. I felt that our nation was becoming more and more human, greater and greater while taking this picture in front of a new government building in Chengdu.

After coming back I read many stories about what had happened in the disaster area. Many journalists let survivors describe their feelings over and over again. Many say this disaster brought our nation more cohesion, and inspired more kindness in people's hearts. The original indifference and isolation among people were replaced by compatriotic warmth, and humans became humans again. But as a witness coming from the disaster area, I want people to realize how horrifying it was for tens of thousands of families to disappear in a flash. If it is painful for me to recall my work there, isn't it more painful for people who lost their families and limbs to recall that terrible experience? Thinking of this, I feel that it's a cruel job being a journalist.

**Zhang Hongjiang: The disaster changed many things, including human relationships and many people's view of life.**

I'm not as sensitive as Cui Jun. Maybe it's because I'm older or my reactions are slower. But I trust my judgment on the environment and security. I have never made any mistake in this aspect, that is why I didn't hesitate. when my newspaper ordered me to go directly from Qomolangma to Chengdu and then to the disaster area.

I have had many thoughts since coming back. In the disaster area my work was only interviewing and photographing. It was tough and dangerous without much food or drink, but it was my job, a kind of choice. You choose to be a journalist, so that's your responsibility. You should go to a place where there's an emergency straightaway. If you don't go, who can go? Aren't you supposed to do that? When I came back, someone said: "Zhang Hongjiang, you guys are noble. You went to such a dangerous place." But I replied, "No. If you were me and in my position, you would go too, so you are noble, too." Probably Cui Jun would give the same answer. We are both veteran journalists, and we are excited about having important work to do. We have no time for moral judgments or individual reflection. We are too busy for that.

On the day I came back, my colleagues went to the airport to meet me with flowers. They said I was a hero. I was very happy. Of course I was happy to see them, but it was the first time they had done me such an honor. I said I was not a hero. In fact, I had done nothing except take a few pictures.

But there have been some changes. For example, my wife is different. She has become diligent. She was not so before. Now she arranges our house so well that I'm not used to it. My son has changed, too. Two years and eight months old, he has just begun kindergarten. After I came back, he became a cry baby, always around me. I like him, but I'm not used to his new habits. However, I understood the reason. I had just come back from the disaster area, so they felt I needed more love and care. The disaster, I think, has changed many things, including human relationships and many people's views of life.

Sometimes I think it is a very subtle feeling.

Take the taxi driver Cui Jun told you about as an example. He treated us very kindly. We left our stuff with a stranger, and promised to return to get it back. He saw us off, and said he would give us a welcome-back banquet when we came back, as if he thought we would never come back. But when we did come back, he insisted on inviting us to a good meal. We left each other with reluctance, and I thought he was the symbol of many people's changed mind-set. They felt guilty about their inability to go to the disaster area to help other people and do something for them, so they tried to treat the people who took part in the rescue activities with care. It is an indirect contribution. Many people made cash and material donations just because they wanted to do their best, given that they couldn't go there in person. At the thought of those people I'm very touched. It is always the case that a disaster is the touchstone of conscience, and once this conscience is stimulated into a general mood of society, what a big harvest we will reap!

Cui Jun has told you many moving stories. He is more emotional than I am.

When we set off from Yingxiu that day, if he hadn't insisted on staying the night in the bus, I would have tried to keep going. My instinct told me that nothing would happen. At the time I was very eager to see the real scene. We were going in the opposite direction to the refugees. Our road got narrower and narrower, and the noise of falling rocks and heavy rain was heard all the time. Nobody knew what was happening or how many people had died ahead of us. We knew that few people from the outside had managed to get through, and that the rescue activities were being carried on by local people. There were problems with everything—food, water, power, communications. I took a maritime satellite telephone with me, so I was able to publish local news to realize news communication as soon as possible. I think that was all we could do.

The night in the bus seemed very long. Now I think Cui Jun was right. Our equipment was not good enough, so it was too dangerous to go at night; besides, we two needed more hands, but our partners insisted on going the next morning. So we could only stay in the bus. The man from Hangzhou who went with us to look for his wife and child was very anxious. Later on, when we met him again in Yingxiu he was happy again, for his wife and child were both safe. They had hidden under a steel cot in a collapsed house, and avoided getting injured. Before he returned to Chengdu he left us all his cigarettes, and hugged us one by one. "I'm so lucky," he said. I was cheered by his mood, and took many pictures of him and his family. After he left, I thought how lucky he had been. In Yingxiu we met lots of people looking for their families. Some of them failed to find them, and some only found the bodies of their relatives. I can't describe their sorrow, sadness and disappointment.

In the disaster area touching stories happened almost every moment. These stories were about life and death, so they touched the soul. What we saw most there were injured people, dead bodies and ruins. There were aftershocks every day, and rain was frequent. During the last few days there was a smell of dead bodies in the air. It was indescribable; I had never smelled it before. I like taking pictures that bring hope of life, and I really felt the power of life emanating from many survivors and badly injured people in the disaster area— the strong and unbending yearning for life. I think this is an active and eternal aspect of human nature, and should be recorded.

I want to give two examples. They are of two people who moved me very much.

One of them was a man over fifty who worked in Yingxiu. When I was taking pictures of a rescue team someone asked me: "Are you a journalist?" I replied, "Yes, I am." He then said, "Then you should interview that man," pointing to a man of very ordinary appearance working with the rescue team. "He started rescuing people after the earthquake before any professional rescue team arrived. He isn't local, and has no relatives here. He could have left like many others, but he didn't." From then on I began to pay attention to the man. He was still there working busily when we left Yingxiu. I think he was a great person, and worth our attention. He certainly knew that it was dangerous to stay, but he stayed. This is a nice aspect of human nature, and one that modern people are gradually losing.

The other was a woman, the subject of one of my pictures. I saw her searching in the ruins of a tottering building. Finally, she found what she was looking for—a pair of earrings. I took a picture of her as she was putting them on. I didn't know her name, and she seemed to be not very young, but her finding the earrings and putting them on really moved me. I thought she was very beautiful, though under her feet was a ruin. I like this picture very much because I see sincere love and eagerness for life and happiness in it. Maybe life is vulnerable in the face of disaster, but as long as we are alive or have hope for life, we can always go for a better and more beautiful life. It is a spiritual power and emotion that enable people to progress. I think that epiphany was a fresh touch of sunshine in the cloudy and gloomy disaster area during that period.

Because of this realization, I don't think my interviews in the disaster area were grey and depressing. The conditions there were really heart-breaking and terrible, but I think we should have the rationality to tell ourselves that since the disaster did occur, we who were left alive should live on and acquire the courage to rebuild our homes. This courage is not given to us by others. It is a strong belief in every heart. Media workers have the responsibility to help people regain this belief. So, since returning from the disaster area I am not willing to read sentimental reports, especially those containing journalists' tears. I understand they are kind people and also were appalled when they saw the terrible disaster, but media workers should be the first to become rational. Tears never save lives, just as tears never return lost loved ones and homes to people in the disaster area. What we can do is more than shed tears.

## Interviewer's Notes

### Black Is Also a Color of Dreams

It was very windy the day I interviewed Cui Jun. Seeing him coming in the distance, I noticed that his hair was no longer long. When he smiled, his chin was very prominent.

He seemed nervous when we began our conversation. He emphasized again and again that he was normal, but his hands were trembling when he pressed the computer keys to show me his pictures. Maybe it was because all the pictures were so grey, and many showed shrouded corpses and broken limbs, and ruined buildings. I dared not ask what he felt when he gazed through the camera lens at those sad sights, but I know it was a special way of looking at the world required by his profession and work, and right now is no doubt the moment for testing his soul.

When I heard Cui Jun mentioning body identification, I was distressed. I was not ready to listen to his memories, and then the pictures before me became vague. I thought I was being cruel to force him to tell what he was not ready to.

Then silence took up more time than words. During this silence, his pictures became a stream of suffering before my eyes.

Once is enough, I thought, and this would be the only time of my life to have this opportunity.

Two days later I interviewed Zhang Hongjiang, who went through many dangers together with Cui Jun. He had the same haggard look as Cui.

Cui Jun and Zhang Hongjiang are both excellent journalists. Their dreams are both related to what they witnessed. What they witnessed might be black, but black is also a color of dreams.

Their experiences have a structure similar to that of the Japanese story "Rashomon"—the same history, the same story and the same disaster left different impressions on different people. After the tears are dried and calm returns to the souls, what is forever unforgettable? Maybe the answers are different.

# *I Live to Make Your Dream More Beautiful*

**Time of interview**: November 8 and 17, 2008.

**Place**: International Hotel, Shijiazhuang.

Luo Jiajia, female, born in Shanghai in 1978. In 1990, her mother remarried in Shijiazhuang so she followed her there. In 1996 she was accepted by a medical college in Hebei Province. In 2001 she went to Germany for graduate study, and in 2006 she got married and settled down in Munich.

**The thing I want to do most when I grow up is to let Mum lead a happy life in old age. I'm not qualified to say I have done that, but at least I have begun, and we have made a good start.**

I really don't know any woman with a sadder fate than Mum. I mean her hard experiences, but from another angle, she is very happy, I think. She has such a rich love experience. Someone loved her so much and was willing to realize her dream as his own. And, what's more important, she has me. I am the one who has lived with her through her lifetime.

I can feel something very strong in her, that is, a woman must support and rely on herself. My mother has put this rule into practice all her life, and she also teaches it to me. The thing I want to do most when I grow up is to give her a happy old age. I'm not qualified to say I have done that, but at least I have begun, and we have made a good start.

I don't know yet the gender of the child I am pregnant with. If it's a boy, I will respect my husband's idea and let him receive his education in Germany.

If it's a girl, I will bring her up together with Mum. I hope she has the strong character of Mum and me. From Mum, I believe firmly that men should be educated by women, though it is hard for women to do that. But it is a must and should be a tradition passed down from generation to generation. Without highly qualified women there can be no highly qualified children or nation or society with high moral and cultural standards. I don't think I am being too extreme or narcissistic.

The story of Mum and I is one about women's self-education and self-help. I'm not exaggerating.

Mum is from Shijiazhuang. Her parents were both connected with medicine. My maternal grandfather was born into a traditional Chinese medical doctor's family, and my maternal grandmother was a pharmacist all her life. They hoped Mum could study medicine and become a doctor, in Mum's words, to heal the world with medical finesse. But she failed them. Far from becoming a doctor, she became a tailor in a residential area. When I was 19, she rented a small shop. Her shop had clothes and lengths of cloth hanging on the walls. Beside the window was a big desk, and on the desk was an electric iron, chalk, needles and thread, scissors, and a tape measure. In the center of the room was an old Bee sewing machine with its paint peeling off. The small shop wasn't returned to its owner until I got married. Before that, I took my German husband to the shop to help her pack the stuff she wanted to keep. I said, "See? It's her hands sewing in this room that enabled me to study in Germany." My husband is not from a rich family. In fact his family is a blue-collar one, though his country is richer than mine. He used to earn money for tuition as a child. He said he respected my mum, for she was honest and hardworking, and all honest labor was worth respect. After we left Mum and returned home that day, I said, "She is more than honest and hardworking; if anyone else had experienced what she experienced, he or she might not be able to survive." This happened more than two years ago, and at the time I suddenly thought of you. I know my mum has been a fan of yours for about ten years. She likes your books and has collected all of them. I have read them, too, but we never shared our ideas about them. I wanted to find you, tell you our story and let you write it down as a memorial of our life. If a mother must give a hundred percent to bring up a child, then a single mother must give two hundred percent, for she has to bear what a father should bear; and if a mother happens to be without a good job, good salary or good parents, she must give more than three hundred percent. My mum is such a woman. Each woman grows out of a little girl having a fantasy which might be related to career, love, family or children. I used to ask her from what time I began to be her only dream.

On the evening when I told Mum that An Dun was coming to listen to our story, she was very quiet. She said, "Well, you tell her. She has a daughter, and she understands."

I have a maternal uncle who was apprenticed to my maternal grandpa. Now he's a famous traditional Chinese medical doctor in Hong Kong. Grandpa has passed away, and Grandma lives together with my maternal uncle. Grandpa didn't call Mum and me to the hospital until he was dying. Grandma used to give us some money behind his back. They thought all the bad luck originated from the man Mum married. But Mum refused to listen to them, and went her own way, which led to many worse things. I used to think Mum didn't accept others' comments on her and her love choice, but many years later when I faced my marriage choice, Mum told me not to make a bad one. Judging from her words, she must have agreed to the idea of my grandparents in those days. She might be a little regretful, but life is short. It's too late when you want to correct your mistakes.

Mum had no chance to go to college when she was young, but she was well educated at home by my grandpa. As a result, she wasn't forced by the environment of that era to be a peasant or worker. She went to a small hospital, and worked there in a traditional Chinese medical pharmacy. In those days, it was a very good job for a woman with only a senior high school diploma.

It was a good start. Sometimes I think if Mum's life were a novel, the good start would be closely related to a romantic and beautiful girl living in peace, and everything would go on smoothly. But it's also possible that a turning point occurs, and the things which follow might not be that perfect. In Mum's novel, a person appeared after the good start, and he is my father. Because of his appearance, many subsequent things weren't that good. He damaged Mum's life that should have been very peaceful and he also entangled me, too. Of course that's the angle of the novel's readers. From the angle of ourselves, our life was destroyed. Every coin has two sides that supplement each other.

When Mum was working in the pharmacy, a Shanghai man came to train at the hospital. In those days, a doctor from outside had to return to his or her hometown after working in the hospital for a while. He was attracted to Mum, and it was a pity that Mum had the same feeling for him. He was six years older than she was.

Within six months they became lovers, and when he had to leave Shijiazhuang Mum was determined to marry him, which my grandparents were strongly against. There were said to be a few reasons. First they looked down upon the man's family: He was a college student, his parents were both senior workers admired by all at that time, and he had four older sisters, three of whom were textile workers and one worked in a gas station. But I don't look down upon them, for to look down upon them meant to look down upon myself. They thought a girl brought up in a literary family couldn't marry into such a family. Second, they were Shanghai natives, against whom my grandparents had a prejudice. They thought they lived differently from northerners. Third, my grandparents didn't think it good for my parents to live so far from each other, and they didn't like the idea of seeing their daughter go to Shanghai with him.

Mum refused to take her parents advice. She chose to break with her parents in order to marry the man. Mum never told me much about it herself, but over the years she told me many fragments, holding herself up as a negative example to me. I assembled them together and began to know how I came into the world after the love story took place.

That was the background in which I grew up. I know what is cheating, what is swallowing an insult, what troubles a widow may have and what it is to be looked down upon by snobs. I know if one doesn't have an insight into people, his or her love affairs will be a miserable failure.

Mum is stubborn, which makes me admire her, but also heart-broken. Let me tell you what happened the last time I saw my grandma before my maternal uncle took her to Hong Kong. After hearing the story, you will probably understand what happened to Mum.

My grandma said I had a lot in common with Mum, but I am more rational or pragmatic, so maybe I can live an easier life than Mum. Grandma asked me to take good care of Mum, for she had had a difficult life.

I remember once Grandma told me Mum was different from me, as she had lived in a superior family, and so she never knew how to protect herself or how evil the world was. She was told fairytales, and thought that a prince on a white horse would come to marry her, but she didn't know that love was only the start, let alone that she should try to get what she wanted or deserved when love was still fresh. Neither did she know that, without the support of a husband, even a queen has to do everything herself—making the fire, cooking, taking care of children and washing diapers, etc. It was impossible for intellectual parents with a sense of superiority to teach her these things; it would have been strange if she had not had bad luck. I am different. When I was young I saw my parents fight. Dad insulted Mum, and he even fooled around with another woman. Finally Mum left him, and married my stepfather, a kind man who cherished Mum. I then had a proper family, and we began to live a poor but harmonious life. But all of a sudden, he died, and everything fell onto Mum's shoulders again. The kind man was gone in a flash. I saw how desperate Mum was. She became a tailor to support the family, and she used her needle and thread to send me to Germany to study medicine. What hard days! That was the background in which I grew up. I know what is cheating, what is swallowing an insult, what troubles a widow may have and what it is to be looked down upon by snobs. I know if one doesn't have an insight into people, his or her love affairs will be a miserable failure.

When I was saying all this, Grandma kept silent. After I had vented my anger, she shed copious tears. I believe she loves Mum with all her heart. How couldn't she love her daughter? She stretched her thin hands out to me and said my words had made her heart-broken. I said, "Don't be like this. I'm fine, and Mum is all right as long as I am. So go to Hong Kong with Uncle. I will take Mum abroad. This is a goal I must reach, and I will tell whoever wants to marry me that he must accept Mum too; otherwise he can go away. So don't expect Mum to take care of you till you pass away." Hearing this, Grandma cried more sadly. She said I was right in spite of my bold words. I said, "If you are a parent again in the next life, don't forget to tell your daughter what real life is, and a man on a white horse isn't necessarily a prince. There is only one prince, who lives very far away, and he might be disabled and can never leave his palace. A girl from an average family often dreams she can meet a kind man. His horse isn't borrowed, and he can bring her a peaceful life, which is more realistic than a romantic start." Grandma said, "How come you are so realistic? Where's the fun in your life?" I pulled my hands back, and told her: "Don't worry about me. My life will be rich because I know what I want, and it isn't something temporary but something that I can enjoy all my life. If it is not, I will refuse it. If I can get what I want, how can my life be tedious? No way. "

Grandma finally left in tears that day. She left some money and other things to me to give to Mum. She said it was bad karma. That word, I think, is preferred by many old people when they are about to pass away. She said her mistake had led to Mum's misery, and Mum's misery had led to me becoming such a twisted girl. So it was bad karma. I didn't like her to say so. I said, "Forget it. I think it is fine. Indeed Mum has had many miseries, but they will end when I grow up. In some sense her miseries give me impetus and a goal, and bad things therefore will become good ones. " Grandma shook her head: "You're too young to understand. I'm not worried about you. You are fine, so I'm not worried. I think if everything could start over again your mum could live a better life, and if she had had a happy marriage you wouldn't be like this. " I laughed, and said: "Old lady, you still don't understand. If Mum had had a happy marriage, I would be living in fairy tales waiting for a false prince, the same as what Mum did when she was young. The horse of the prince is borrowed. Before he kidnapped and sold me he would make me pregnant. If that happened, my life would be bitter. You will understand because of your old age, won't you? One can live a pragmatic life if he or she sees through all the realistic things in life at an early date. There's no surprise in the world. I don't want to be an innocent girl like Mum used to be. I like the way I am. "

Grandma kept shaking her head and sighing. Maybe it was because she didn't understand, or maybe it was because of her pride in being an intellectual. Time would never go backwards anyway, and she could change nothing.

Now that you know the background, it will be easier for you to understand our life. In a word, Mum's love experiences were like those of the daughters from rich families in TV operas who elope with workers, and whose fates suffer a dramatic decline.

In fact I'm not clear about most details of Mum's love experiences. All I know is the impact of her experiences on our life. Chinese mothers often claim to be friends of their children, but few of them can really be so, which is very typical of our national character. What do you think? Our nation is introverted and autistic, or implicit. My husband said that was depressing, but that's what we are. Will you tell your daughter in detail about your feeling when you fall in love, get married or divorce? I'll bet you won't.

Probably one day your mum will tell you of her heart's journey in those years. If you can write it down, I'll read it. I want to read about my mum through others' words or records. It sounds abnormal, but in fact it couldn't be more normal. That's our way of life, and the way we express our emotions. Chinese parents and children have been doing this since long, long ago.

I guess Mum's problem was that she had no family. It was very difficult for her to go back to Shijiazhuang with me, so she would rather swallow Dad's insults. At least that way I had both Mum and Dad. However, she met a guy totally free of a sense of responsibility.

Continuing with our life.

The most important life decision Mum made that year was to go to Shanghai with that man. Was it a mistake from the very beginning? I can't or shouldn't say so, but I think it was something of a mistake. The man said that after arriving in Shanghai he would find Mum a job. He must have painted a wonderful picture, which prevented Mum regretting leaving home.

Only a month after their marriage, Mum got pregnant. At the time Mum's work records were still in Shijiazhuang, which would not do. So they had to be transferred to Shanghai, where Mum got a job in a cafe.

I was born in Shanghai. My earliest memory about Mum was that she was good at dressing me up. She made me clothes, knitted me sweaters, combed my braids for me, sewed my bag and sent me to school. Everyone said I was beautiful. It wasn't me, but Mum's care. Other memories about her were that the man had bad relations with Mum, who had even worse relations with his family. Mum is a northerner. Despite coming from a much better family than that of the man, Mum was still despised by them. They thought Mum and I were bumpkins. Mum was very beautiful, but she was still a cafe worker, while the man gradually became somebody—head of a surgical department.

That man, I mean my real father, left a deep impression on me, which didn't vanish until Mum and I moved into a small house of a narrow alley. The cafe lent the house to her after she got divorced. In my memory, the man was very fashionable. He wore suits, used hair pomade, and carried a leather satchel. He wore polished shoes and white shirts. He changed his clothes and watches very frequently. Finally he even changed his wife. The woman had left her parents to be with him and had given him a daughter.

In my memory he was a cheater. He often deceived Mum and me. He stayed out at night on the excuse of night duty. He often stayed at his parents' on the excuse that he was ill and didn't want to infect me. What was more difficult to understand was that his parents and sisters helped him deceive us right to the end, when he got another woman and was able to remarry after divorcing Mum. Anyway, he was waiting for Mum to agree to a divorce and take me away.

All children are foolish. I think all men and women who deceive children for the sake of their affairs are degrading. If one day I have an affair I won't deceive my child. I knew the woman he took home, very thin and tall. They talked in Shanghai dialect. I can speak Shanghai dialect, but Mum doesn't. The woman wore a white one-piece dress with white lace borders. Mum sold breakfast every morning, and then she and her co-workers sat and made fried steamed bread, which Mum would sell at noon and in the afternoon. She was very busy. Sometimes when I was doing my homework at home after school the man and the woman would come. He let me call her aunt. The so-called aunt would give me money to go out and buy what I wanted. I always went very far away, and hung around Waibaidu Bridge and the City God Temple, and didn't come back until the money was gone. When I came back they had usually left. Half an hour after the street lights came on Mum would come back. I really can't continue. What a degrading couple they were! They did it on the floral bed sheet Mum had washed. So sordid!

I've never asked Mum whether she knew about their affair. No wife, I think, is unaware of this kind of thing. Those wives who don't mention it or get angry must have their own problems. I guess Mum's problem was that she had no family. It was very difficult for her to go back to Shijiazhuang with me, so she would rather swallow Dad's insult. At least in this way I had both Mum and Dad.

I always think we met a very irresponsible man. He offered to divorce first, for he said he didn't have much in common with Mum. He said she had no ambition and was satisfied with her current job. He forced Mum to divorce because there was another woman waiting for him.

At that time Mum often wept, holding me in her arms. When she was washing vegetables, cooking, walking or lying in bed, she would suddenly begin to cry for no reason. I think all children become grown up at a special moment. I did. I grew up overnight when Mum encountered this incident. I moved away with her. The man never visited us. He gave Mum 80 yuan every month till I was 18. But he paid us the whole sum at one time. I thought he was so rich. Later, Mum told me that his family had raised the money to sever their relationship with us.

From then on, there was only Mum and myself in our family.

**When I saw in a film a boy waiting for a girl on a snowy day, I often thought of Dad. He is the person waiting for me in the snow holding an overcoat, gloves and scarf, and he can move me more than any boy. He's my step-father!**

In fact, I was brought up by my step-father. Whenever I mention my biological father, I call him natural father, or that man, or call him by his name. My step-father is my real father.

When I was ten, Mum met Dad. He was a buyer for a market in Shijiazhuang. He went on a business trip in Shanghai every month. The hotel he stayed in was near Mum's cafe, where he often had breakfast. They two shared the same dialect, and gradually they got to know each other.

I have no idea how they fell in love. One day, Mum took me to meet him, and he took a lot of pictures of us all with his big camera, which has perhaps become an antique now. Then Mum asked me whether I was willing to leave Shanghai. I told her I was willing to follow her wherever she went. Mum said, "Well, let's go back to our hometown." It was one of the most important decisions she made. She moved back to Shijiazhuang with me.

From the first day we arrived in Shijiazhuang from Shanghai we began to live in Dad's house, where Mum is still living. She arranged the house with her own hands. On the wall hung pictures of Dad and Mum. I had my own room. I studied in a primary school nearby, and Dad didn't go out on business any more. I called him Dad right from the start, because I knew they were married. Mum's husband is my Dad, right? What's more, he was kind to me, much kinder than that other man.

When everything settled down, I was already 12.

From then on Mum never had a formal job. She became a tailor, and at first our house served as her workshop.

In others' eyes Dad wasn't a talented person, but he carried the burden of our life on his shoulders. He got a lot of business for Mum's workshop, like uniforms for market salesmen, hotel bed sheets and pillowcases, neighbors' clothes, and those of Dad's co-workers and their families and friends. Mum was hard working, and Dad was very popular, so our clients never refused to pay. Sometimes they gave us food and everyday items instead of money.

Dad treated me very well. It was his first marriage, so they could have another baby, but they didn't do that, for Dad said I was the only child of the family.

Dad's work was hard, but he never fell asleep whenever Mum burned the midnight oil. And the next morning he would take me to school. Later, I had to attend night classes for the graduation examination, and he always picked me up on his bicycle whatever the weather. If the weather suddenly turned cold, he would bring warm clothes for me. I saw in a film a boy waiting for a girl in the snow. It reminded me of Dad. He was the person waiting for me in the snow holding an overcoat, gloves and scarf, and he can move me more than any boy. He's my step-father!

Due to my parents' hard work, we were a very harmonious family. I did very well at school, so they didn't need to worry about me. At the time my ideal was to enter a college, get a good job, and bring them a better life and happy days in their old age.

In others' eyes, perhaps, Mum was really unlucky because she met that man and was insulted despite her hard work in Shanghai. However, I think she has her own happiness, because she met Dad. Definitely, Dad was deeply in love with Mum; otherwise how could he give up his right to have a baby for the sake of another's child?

Dad came from an ordinary family. My grandparents were both workers, and I had an uncle working in Shaanxi Province. They were all kind people, and treated Mum and me very well. After Dad was gone, Uncle still regarded me as his own niece, and Mum as his sister-in-law. He was a merchant, and could be considered a rich man. Mum did her tailoring work to make money for my college tuition and expenses for my study abroad. Out of sympathy, Uncle gave us much help. When I was leaving Shijiazhuang for Germany, my uncle and aunt came to see me off. Mum thanked them and let me thank them. Uncle wept. He said his brother's (Dad's) ideal was Mum and I could be happy. Also, he said, whoever his brother liked was a member of his family.

Sometimes, I do think Mum had a bad fate. Finally, she met a good man, but Dad died the year I entered college. From when he was diagnosed with cancer to his death, it was less than two months. In his last days he wasn't tortured by much pain, and somebody said it was because he was a kind man and had been doing good deeds all his life, so God favored him and kept pain away from him. The doctor told us earlier that cancer would bring great pain in the end, but he was gone after only one injection of Demerol. His last expression was peaceful. He told Mum and me what he wanted to say. He said to me: "You're grown up. Promise me you'll take care of Mum from now on. She is a child of nature, and nobody is more innocent than she is in the world. Now I entrust her to you. You must make the evening of her life a happy one. " He said to Mum: "Take care of our child. Work another few years to realize her dream. She wants to go abroad, so let her do it. She is an independent child. She will have a better life path than we had. You didn't realize your dream of becoming a doctor, so let her realize it for you. " All this time, I was weeping. So was Mum. She lowered her head to Dad's hand. Dad wiped her tears away. That was his last movement, and in my memory at the time Mum was as if in his arms.

My dream had been to take them to my home after I got a diploma, a good job and a good salary abroad. Then Dad was gone, and my dream died too. My new goal was to keep my mother with me forever.

I was able to earn my own tuition as a private teacher. In our house traces of Dad and Mum's living together were everywhere as if Dad were only away on business. Once, when Dad failed to pick me up after night classes for a few days, my classmates asked: "Where's your dad?" I answered, "He has gone away on business. " I always think that Dad will pick me up when he gets back in a few days, and I will see the light of his bicycle shining in the distance, exactly the same as before. Although there was no blood relationship between us, and we had quite different educational backgrounds, my very first love for a man, I think, was for Dad. Without Dad, Mum and I wouldn't have our present life.

Mum shut the door of her heart after Dad was gone. She had no feelings for anyone except me. She became vegetarian, and began to believe in Buddhism. I know Dad took her love away with him.

From then on, I determined to bring Mum happiness whatever happened. But my goal wasn't clear, for I didn't know what happiness really was. What I knew was that Mum should quit her tailoring job and stop working hard for me. I wanted her to spend my money, not the other way round.

I had been looking forward to studying abroad, and it was also Dad's wish. On the first day of college, Dad took me to school. He said, "Listen. Study for the sake of your parents, so try to be outstanding; we will give everything for your tuition, and we hope one day you will go abroad to study and be an excellent doctor. If you can make it, Mum won't regret her lifetime of hard work. " At that time, as if in a dream, I looked forward to the day when I could take them to my place after I got a diploma, a good job and a good salary abroad. Then Dad was gone, and my dream died. I gradually got a very specific goal, that is, to have my mother with me forever.

Probably I was the hardest working among my classmates. I'm not talking big. Studying and working as a private teacher took up all my time every day. I had no amusement during college, and never indulged myself. Others were in love, and some boys were chasing me, but I knew they were not my ideal men. I needed one that could accept my background and additional conditions, and could help me realize my dream. I'm utilitarian, right? It's because my ideal was quite simple.

During the last year of college, many classmates began to plan for further study abroad. Though at the time the overseas educated were no longer that sought-after, they could still have a good job and better pay. One day Mum said, "You can go abroad. I have 200,000 yuan, but that's all I have. " I was shocked. She was only a tailor, an old widow who could barely support our family with constant hard work. How did she get so much money? Mum sat at the sewing machine, and raised her head, "Some of it was left by your dad and me, some came from your uncle, some came from your father's organization, and some was saved by your dad and me for this day to come to realize your dream. " I still remember her words. I said, "Mum, I will repay you double. "

With that big sum of money Mum gave me I went to Germany and began studying abroad in 2001.

We all know how hard life is for an overseas student. I don't think there is anything to talk about. I knew I was poor, so I had to study hard to get more chances to earn money and get a diploma. No matter whether you stay or go back to China, good grades and professional quality decide whether you can get a good job. There are two kinds of overseas students. Some of them are from rich families, and studying abroad only means enjoyment to them. After spending some time at school and getting overseas experience and enough credits they will definitely have a good future, for money can buy anything. I belong to the other kind, who use their family's money for study abroad just to get a genuine diploma, which is the key factor for them to change their fate. The life dream of the poor is no longer to be poor, right? So work hard, grab every chance you get and use all your energy!

I did work hard, for I knew a tailor's daughter had no other choice, and I couldn't keep my promise to Dad that I would give happiness to Mum until I got out of poverty.

In Germany I got several love chances. Some of them were Chinese, while others were foreigners. Maybe I was too pragmatic; whenever they told me they loved me and wanted a deeper relationship I would tell them that I wanted to bring Mum with me, and tell them our basic conditions and why I wanted to do this. If they didn't accept that, I told them, they were just wasting their time, for we were all busy studying and making a living. It was a waste of time to do something without a result. I wasn't romantic, right? No. I wasn't qualified, and I didn't expect romance either. I thought Mum had been hurt badly by romance, so I didn't want to repeat the process. In front of such a pragmatic woman, they were afraid and ran off. No big deal. I didn't mind, for I thought I could meet someone who could accept me. There was no big problem even if I couldn't, for I could live by myself.

In 2004 I met my present husband. He had just divorced, and had a child. As my tutor's friend, he met me at my tutor's house. He dated me first, and the love process lasted for more than one year, for we had too much to talk about but few chances to meet. I was lucky this time. When I finally told him about everything that had happened to Mum, he said, "Bring your Mum here to live with us!" I knew then that I had met my Mr. Right.

I know many people can't understand me. Is there only reality between a man and a woman? No love? I would only develop my love on the premise that the man accepts my conditions. I'm different from Mum, who was driven by crazy love and had no idea that she would end up working in a cafe. I'm not criticizing her. What I want to say is that women of her generation were victims of novels produced in the 18th and 19th centuries. They wanted nothing but love. We are quite different. We put material in the first place and then spirit! Love is not food, and men are not life-long support.

In 2005 I came back to Shijiazhuang for the first time. I told Mum that I was going to marry a German who loved me very much, and we planned to take her to live with us.

When she found out that my husband was divorced and had a child, she was shocked. For about two days she kept busy and silent. She made me a red silk cheongsam, as I asked. On the third evening she cooked my favorite braised chestnuts and chicken. We had dinner sitting opposite each other, and when it came to the second bowl she said, "Don't make a mistake for my sake. I'm living here happily. I don't want to go abroad. It's not necessary for you to take me abroad. Don't think that would be good for me. "

That was the longest conversation we ever had, but I only told her half of what I wanted to. I had chosen such a man to take her abroad, and at first I really thought that was my only purpose. But later I found I loved him, for he loved me so much that he made me think it a crime not to love him back. In this sense I didn't sacrifice my love; it was just that I combined love and profit very well. I was lucky. "Dad is gone, and I know you two have the most intense love in the world, though I don't know how you fell in love with each other. Without Dad, your heart is a dead one. But he is really gone. Don't deceive yourself. You're living alone, and it's a long time from now to when you get together with him. During this period I want you to be with me. I promised Dad I would take care of you till you two get together. To bring me up has been your dream. Now I'm grown up, and to take good care of you is one of my dreams," I said.

Was I being cruel? I don't think so. An adult should be courageous enough to face reality. It's not being cool. It's being rational.

That night I heard her sobbing. I knew what she was thinking.

In 2006 I got married in the cheongsam Mum had made me, and began to live in Munich. Before that my husband and I came to Shijiazhuang to take Mum to our wedding, and we took away the biggest and most handsome picture of Dad, which is hanging in the room we prepared for Mum.

The story of Mum and me should stop here. Of course, compared with the past decades, the story is too simple. I don't know what Mum would think if she read this one day. There are many things Mum never knew, such as my firm determination in those years. Whatever she thinks, I hope she believes that I love her very much, and her happiness is mine, for she took my happiness as her life goal.

*Some Words One Would Never Want to Tell*

On the third afternoon after the interview, I e-mailed Luo Jiajia my completed story, with the following letter:

Dear Luo Jiajia,

Thanks for the trust of you and your husband, and thank you for the chance to get close to your mum. When I was writing the story, many times my eyes were so full of tears that I had to pause for a moment to see the computer screen clearly. Your warm story gave me a chance to get to know a great woman. Thanks. I think my readers will know more when they share her love experiences, just as I do.

Good luck!

Yours sincerely,

An Dun

At about nine o'clock on the same evening I received a call from Luo Jiajia. She said she hoped the story would not be published, for her mum didn't want her to hurt others with her memories.

"Could you tell me who would be hurt?" I asked imprudently.

"That man. We both know who it is," she answered.

That day we talked for hours on the phone. She repeated again and again that it was her mother's wish, not hers. As regards herself, she said, "It doesn't matter to me. I hope everyone understands Mum and knows what kind of person my biological dad was. I promise that what I said about him reflected my own thoughts and the reality in those days. I'm not libeling him, but I couldn't beautify him, either, for he really doesn't deserve it. "

She apologized to me, for she thought I had gone all the way to Shijiazhuang for nothing. I said I could understand her mum, for I knew her feelings well.

"You know? How do you know?" she said. She didn't believe me.

"I know maybe you hate that man and hope his bad deeds will be exposed, but your mum would never want to do that, because you never loved him but she was in love with him for many years, and you were the fruit of that relationship," I said.

When I put the phone down I felt really depressed, not about the efforts I had made, but because I thought that such a good story might be covered up. Looking at the manuscript I felt regretful.

Early on the morning of November 17, I decided to try to persuade them.

Setting off at half past five in the morning from Beijing, I arrived at Shijiazhuang before nine. On my way, I was constantly thinking: Life is really like a movie.

When Luo Jiajia heard that I was in Shijiazhuang she was greatly surprised. Half an hour later, she sat in my car and cried. Another half an hour later, I was eating breakfast her mum had made in her tiny living room.

We spent a whole morning in front of the computer correcting the manuscript word by word. Before going out, her mum told me: "You know, my daughter said all this, and it is her right to do so. She didn't lie. I didn't say what I would never want to tell all my life, you know. "

So when you, my readers, read this story, you will know that this is neither the original love story of the old lady, nor the sorrowful story reminding me of the theme song of *Sad Movie*. No.

But I kind of like the present story. I like the young woman telling the story and like her rationality with a touch of spite, for I know that is what I lack. I even envy her a little. She is nearer to steadiness and happiness because she is rational, if steadiness means happiness.

I miss another story I stayed up and wrote down after I returned to Beijing from Shijiazhuang on November 8, and miss the woman who has a totally pure dream over which she is torn apart. She is already old. Another portion of her that I didn't see or hear has become a miracle due to her nearly-completed life. Without her miracle, of course, her daughter would not be able to have her present life. Maybe it is something inevitable that every generation of women must experience—we often come from afar along the track of the past generation with stumbling steps.

# I Choose to Change Your Life

**Time of interview**: May 20, 2008

**Place**: Starbucks Coffee, Beijing World Trade Center

Su Shifeng was born in Henan Province in 1962, and had been working in Shenzhen since 1978. He began to do volunteer work in Shenzhen in 2000. He joined the Shenzhen Anti-drug Education Group in 2001, and was lauded as a "Five-star Volunteer in Shenzhen" in 2003. Su came to Beijing the same year, and worked as the general manager of Oumasite Beijing Art Wall & Decoration Materials Co. Ltd. He then became a city volunteer for the Beijing Olympic Games and an anti-drug volunteer for the capital. Su set up a "family hotline for addicts" in 2007 to offer free services to help people give up drugs. He has also been active in promoting knowledge of AIDS prevention and control, and has adopted three AIDS orphans. He has donated over 5,000 milliliters of blood in Shenzhen and Beijing since 2000. Su wrote a book titled *A Psychological Counseling Manual for the May 12th Wenchuan Earthquake* soon after the earthquake. He had 10,000 copies printed at his own expense and delivered them to the disaster-hit area himself on May 26.

**I do not want to say how noble I am; I just want you to realize that being a volunteer makes my life beautiful and amazing.**

I first became a volunteer in Shenzhen. Do you know anything about that city? I'd been living there for over two decades. It is a very young, energetic and modern city, with migrants from various provinces. The city is growing at a fantastic speed. My wife was a native of Shenzhen, and my daughter was born there. My career also started there. Actually, I thought of Shenzhen as my second hometown. Yet it is also a place that broke my heart. I divorced in 2002, as I could not get along with my wife. My daughter stayed there with her mother, and I came to Beijing alone. I wanted to leave Shenzhen to start a brand-new life.

I'm telling you this just to let you know how I became a volunteer. I don't want to say how noble I am; I just want you to realize that being a volunteer makes my life beautiful and amazing. Volunteer work actually offers me new hopes and enhances my morality. I also feel that, besides supporting a family, I am a useful person to society as a whole.

I worked and lived a stable life in Shenzhen before 2000. I had lots of time, and everything was well organized. There was little entertainment for business people at that time, such as playing *mahjong*, drinking and karaoke, which I was not interested in. I felt so bored during my spare time. Besides, I did not get along well with my wife then, so I was thinking of getting myself a meaningful thing to do.

Frankly, I'm a good-humored person with a kind heart. I studied what volunteers did in many cities at that time. Many people did volunteer work in Shenzhen, such as looking after the elderly and environmental protection. I tried such work while making my own choice, and I finally chose to do what I wanted most and suited me best: I became a volunteer to promote anti-drug education and one-to-one anti-drug help, specifically, making friends with drug abusers and helping them quit drugs.

Have you ever seen a drug user? I always feel that no one really wants to take drugs, but is always pressed to do so. They cannot quit the devastating habit due to a lack of willpower or being ignored and discriminated against by the outside world. Many drug abusers are very upset when they are off drugs. They also want to be good people without bad habits. Yet, you know, it's the most difficult thing to get rid of a psychological addiction. So a trustworthy person is needed to accompany and encourage him to make it. If an anti-drug volunteer can help a person get rid of drug addiction physically and psychologically, the volunteer is actually saving that person's life. A drug addict causes his whole family endless trouble. His parents can do nothing but just watch him take drugs and even commit crimes to pay for drugs. If you had a chance to see them, and listened to their stories of fighting against drugs and watching their children being destroyed by drugs, you would learn that a volunteer who gets a person off drugs actually saves his whole family. I think this is a meaningful thing with merits and virtues, yet full of challenges. It needs love, patience, extensive psychological knowledge, strong communication skills, and a concept of treating others as equals.

Then I offered to be one of the anti-drug volunteers in Shenzhen, which was a very precious and impressive experience for me.

It is well known that drug abusers are vulnerable to HIV Aids. They are always kept at bay by most people, and also bring fear to others. People believe that it's dangerous to have physical contact with drug addicts. Actually, people misunderstand the way AIDS spreads. In fact, those who take drugs are not always AIDS carriers. We also emphasize this point when promoting knowledge of AIDS control and prevention. The first time I worked as a volunteer, however, I could not help worrying about physical contact with them, although I already knew nothing would happen. When looking back now, I feel glad that the drug addict I helped and educated did not know what I thought at that time. If he had felt that, it might have been a big blow to him psychologically, and he might even have despaired. According to my own experience over many years, drug users are very sensitive, vulnerable and fragile. As a disadvantaged group, they place more expectations on others. For instance, they hope to be accepted by the mainstream, not discriminated against. They want trust and support from others, and hope someone can help them quit drugs once and for all.

I offered one-to-one help in Shenzhen, which meant that I had to take the person I served as a friend. He would probably need me at any time—when he was unhappy, when problems occurred in his relationships, etc. Sometimes an addict would be afraid to go into the street. . . . I had to help them deal with all the trifles in their lives. I also had to talk with him constantly to find out what he was thinking about. We were virtually partners in life. Retrospectively, I learned that it was good to be really needed by others. The people I helped trusted me so much that some couldn't help holding my hand, and I always felt that a person with a real desire to quit drugs and return to normal society would not hold my hand if he didn't trust me so much. Actually, what he held was not only the hand of a volunteer, but the hope to return to the mainstream of society. Who can reject such trust? Besides, I also found my own value in this trust.

**Drug addicts who were trying to quit drugs also stayed with us on that day, and we used such a way to tell them that society had not abandoned them; instead, they were welcomed with open arms.**

I came to Beijing in 2003, and suddenly felt very empty. I found the Beijing Volunteers Association through the Internet the day after I arrived. I tried to find whether there was any specific organization for anti-drug volunteers. I finally became an anti-drug volunteer. Unlike Shenzhen, there was no one-to-one help in Beijing at that time. What I could do was to promote knowledge of anti-drug and AIDS control and prevention. A newcomer to Beijing, I still felt the kindness and tolerance of the people of this city during these activities. We once held an activity in Ditan (Temple of Earth) Park, where volunteers were required to wear masks and hold flowers. Each also held a small board with "I am a drug addict. Can you give me a hug?" written on it. If a passer-by gave one a sincere hug, he/she would get a flower. I was really touched that young girls, children with their parents and university students were all ready to embrace them. One little girl did not know what "drug addict" meant. I explained to her, and she smiled and said, "That's all right, if only she could quit. " She then hugged one of the volunteers. Drug addicts who were trying to quit drugs also stayed with us on that day, and we used this method to tell them that society had not abandoned them, but instead, welcomed them with open arms.

We gradually got more experience through such campaigns, with more people joining our volunteer team. We set up a "hotline family for addicts" and

"a ray of hope" in 2007. The names originated from our volunteer experience. Family members of drug addicts always feel very anxious and worried that they will be discriminated against, sneered at or hurt. So they prefer to seek help from strangers, and dial a strange number for help, placing hopes on those strangers who would like to offer help. I deeply understand what they feel. For them, this hotline is a ray of hope that perhaps the volunteers will have a genuine desire to help them. Here I would like to talk about the hotline volunteers. Some of them used to be drug abusers themselves, who have now quit drugs. They have experienced the struggle of life and death, and the process of fighting the temptation of drugs. What they suffered and experienced allows them to be more convincing to drug addicts and their family members. We regularly organize drug addicts with a desire to quit to participate in group activities, asking them to talk about their feelings, lives and psychological difficulties in the process of detoxification. The volunteers who have quit drugs always tell people of their own experiences and the ways they treat themselves psychologically. Experience has proved that this method is really effective. Most participants are self-motivated, and become more confident after these activities. They are convinced that they are able to do things that others have done.

I am particularly proud when drug addicts quit drugs, and became anti-drug volunteers themselves. I feel that they have become born again.

**An amount as little as 1,800 yuan can provide sufficient food, clothing and education for a child. Yet for us, this is not big money, only equivalent to what we pay for a meal when we go out with friends.**

Anti-drug education is closely related to AIDS prevention and treatment. As an anti-drug volunteer, I have had opportunities to learn a lot about AIDS orphans. I adopted two children orphaned by AIDS in 2007. They are brothers. I also helped my daughter raise a little girl orphaned by AIDS this year. All of them are from the Liangshan Yi Autonomous Prefecture, Sichuan.

I first came to know that Liangshan is a place where AIDS is prevalent when I was engaged in education on AIDS prevention and control. Liangshan is not a wealthy place, yet many people there take drugs. When I visited Liangshan I found out that drugs are very cheap there, and it is also a place that produces drugs. The people there have little entertainment, and lead an empty spiritual life. However, although drugs are cheap there, syringes are not, so they tend to share them, and that is how AIDS spreads. AIDS orphans are common. I felt extremely sad after learning what happens in this place. I'm also a father, and I would feel bad if I were in those people's shoes. My child is well educated and enjoys a happy life, yet kids there cannot even have adequate food and clothing, let alone education.... I know that an amount as small as 1,800 yuan can provide sufficient food, adequate clothes and education for a child for one year. Yet for us, this is not big money, sometimes just equivalent to what we pay for a meal when going out with friends.

Thinking of that, I then contacted local volunteers, and said to them, "Could you please help take care of the kids I have adopted? I really hope this modest amount of money can be spent to help make their lives better." The use of the money should be supervised by the local volunteers, as I didn't want the children to squander it and finally followed the tragic road their parents had taken. The local volunteers there were very responsible. They reported to me about the lives and academic performances of the two children regularly. I was always very glad when I was told about the progress they had made. They were very poor. Their father had died of a drug overdose, while their mother had also been an addict and was affected by HIV AIDS. Their mother suddenly disappeared one day. She might even be dead, as her health was ruined. The two brothers were then living together with their grandmother, who had no income. By simply skipping one meal or one carton of cigarettes, you can provide a decent life for someone. Isn't that wonderful?

My daughter is now studying at a university in Shenzhen, and we call each other frequently. I told her what had happened to the two brothers some time ago. She listened to me quietly, and said, "Dad, could you also help me adopt a girl? I would like to donate part of my living allowance to support her. We are living a life of luxury compared to them!" And so, my daughter also became a sponsor of a little girl. They exchange letters regularly, and are now getting along very well.

I believe that young people who, like my daughter grew up in an ordinary family, sometimes need to do something to help others within their ability. They can learn to be selfless and caring, and try to share happiness with others in this process. I hope my daughter can learn more about society in this way.

She should get to know how lucky she is, and learn to return something to society, as I learned from my experience as a volunteer over many years. I hope I can teach my daughter by my personal example and verbal instructions.

My current wife is very supportive of my volunteer work. She says that as I can do good to others without any conditions, I will certainly treat my loved ones better.

I don't know how to say it, but I felt grieved for my daughter when I divorced my wife. We always quarreled at that time, which brought great pressure to my daughter, as she was not a little girl then. Children in single-parent families are always more sensitive, and so was my daughter at that time. She asked me why I divorced her mother. I could not explain to her what had really happened to our adult relationship. As a man, frankly, I would never chose to divorce if it was not impossible to continue to live together.

When my ex-wife learned that I had a new girlfriend, she tried to commit suicide. On that day, I had picked up my daughter to take her to her grandmother's apartment. My daughter told me on the way that her mother had just taken lots of medicine, actually a bottle of pills. I suddenly figured out what had happened, and rushed back to where my wife lived. I found her unconscious. I rushed with her to a hospital, where she was finally revived. I felt extreme suffering at that time. Why did we have to hurt each other, and our child as well? It was roughly at that time that I made my decision to leave Shenzhen.

My ex-wife was not so supportive of my work as a volunteer, and we even argued over this issue. I had no expectations for the future with that much disharmony in our life. I lived alone after I came to Beijing. I hurt my back accidentally, and it was really tough for me at that time. It was too painful for me to stand up, and I could not even get myself a cup of water without someone else's help. Finally I had to creep on all fours into the kitchen. One day, a girl from Sichuan—I hadn't known her long—came to deliver something. When she saw me in that pitiable condition she offered to look after me and help prepare my meals. We became more and more friendly over the following ten days. Just like me, she had also been born and brought up in a poor village. I told her about my experiences of being a volunteer. Later, she became my wife. My current wife is very supportive of my volunteer work. She says that as I can do good to others without any conditions, I will certainly treat my loved ones better. Now we have a five-month-old daughter.

Sometimes I think we should put ourselves in somebody else's position. I take good care of her and her family members, and she does the same for me. My daughter has been living in Beijing with me for two years. My wife treats her very well, and they have become close friends, not like step-mother and step-daughter. More interestingly, my ex-wife's elder sister and my wife have also become good friends. My daughter, after she was enrolled by a university, told me that she had hated me before, as I had left her mother alone. Yet she changed her mind later, and began to understand that everyone needs to pursue happiness. She even said she was proud of what I am doing, and that her father is such a nice person. I felt particularly glad to hear what she said. My girl has already grown up.

If being a volunteer has changed my life, I think that this is an important part of the changes.

## Interviewer's Notes ·····················□

### The Spirit of Volunteerism

The sun shone brightly on the day I interviewed Su Shifeng. When I saw him in the distance sitting in the sunshine, I felt that this tall man with a white volunteer's T-shirt really embodied the phrase "Mens sana in corpore sano" (A healthy mind in a healthy body).

Two things made me feel that Su Shifeng was a person I needed to make friends with, not only a person I needed to interview.

Su Shifeng looked after his father-in-law for a year in 2002, one year before he left Shenzhen, until the old man passed away. Su had divorced his first wife at that time. During a chat with his mother-in-law, the medical staff at the hospital said, "Your son is so filial." The old lady felt sad, and told them in a low voice: "No, he used to be my son-in-law, but he has divorced my daughter." Su Shifeng then became well known in that hospital. I asked him why he did it, and he replied that the old couple had been very nice to him. No matter what had happened between their daughter and him, their relations were not changed or even affected. Su's own parents were no longer living, and so the old couple took Su as their son, and even didn't side with their daughter over the divorce issue. How many parents could do this? The couple also insisted on looking after Su's child to help reduce the psychological impact on the little girl by offering her a comfortable environment. So Su Shifeng was grateful and eager to support the elderly couple for what they had done for his daughter.

Su Shifeng has been walking in the Fragrant Hills every Sunday since he arrived in Beijing in 2003. He was shocked to see the amount of litter that visitors left behind in this renowned beauty spot. So Su began to take a large garbage bag with him every time he went walking there. He says it makes his heart ache to see the way the Fragrant Hills are treated as a dumping ground for garbage. He also had more than 300 notices urging people not to leave litter lying around put up at his own expense. This had some effect, but he still carries a garbage bag with him. "It is wonderful to be able to take exercise while protecting the environment," he said.

He mentioned these two things lightly, just as parts of the interview, yet I was deeply impressed with the facts that he was a qualified volunteer as well as an earnest person.

The day we chatted happened to be the mourning day for the victims of the Wenchuan earthquake. He brought me a printed booklet titled, *Psychological Counseling Manual for the May 12th Wenchuan Earthquake*. He and other volunteers were publishing at their own expense. They were preparing to have 10,000 copies printed and sent to the disaster-hit area. I asked him how much he had spent on this venture, and he replied vaguely, " Not so much. We will continue to print the book regardless of how much it costs. People in the disaster-hit areas really need the book...." Then he shifted to another topic, claiming that he met a very nice person in the course of this venture. The man decided to charge no fees for typesetting and printing once he learned that what they were doing was for the disaster-hit area. "In my view, volunteerism is not a capacity, it is actually some kind of spirit. So long as you help others, serve and pay back something to society, you are a volunteer, and you deserve to be respected," he said. This may be the most heroic thing he said during the whole interview.

I called Su Shifeng on the morning of May 27. He said that he was at the Communist Youth League of Sichuan Province. He left his five-month-old daughter, and went there with the psychological counseling manual. "I'm here to deliver these books, and to see what can be done. I'll just do whatever I can," he said.

"Do whatever I can" became his catch phrase during all our conversations. He said these words when he was busy asking people to donate materials and money to the disaster-hit areas, when he continued to clear away rubbish on every path of the Fragrant Hills, and when he prepared the notices to remind people to protect their shared environment.

Su Shifeng is a qualified volunteer, a trustworthy friend and an "elder brother" respected by many people, yet he cannot be regarded as a good boss. He has spent too much time on volunteer work, and has no extra time and energy to manage his company properly. As time went by, his partner would occasionally complain that the company was close to being closed down due to Su's careless management. But, interestingly, instead of being closed, his company enjoys booming development. Su Shifeng attributes this success to his good luck, and regards himself as a blessed person. As far as I am concerned, his nice personality accounts for this too.

# *The Infinite Landscape*
# *Is Seen While Traveling*

**Time of interview**: August 18, 2006 to October 2008

**Place**: Beijing Cloud and Sky Photo Image Gallery

Yu Yuntian, male, 59, was born in Tai'an, Shandong Province. He graduated from the Tianjin Academy of Arts. He is director of the China Photographers Association and vice-chairman of the Civil Aviation Administration of China (CAAC) Photographers Association. He was once editor-in-chief of *CAAC Magazine*.

From 1997 to 2003, Yu held several photographic exhibitions in the United States, Cuba, and Austria. In recent years, he has been invited to act as judge for many photographic contests at home and abroad.

**At that time when I went to Tianjin Academy of Arts, I wanted to return to drawing, but it seemed that since I loved photography, I couldn't abandon it.**

I came to like photography through drawing. At that time the purpose of taking pictures was for collecting materials for drawing and reference.

During that period, the "cultural revolution" (1966-1976) was raging, and students didn't go to class but "carried out revolution." Because of my bad family background, after I graduated from junior middle school, I was not assigned a job, so I stayed at home, playing basketball, learning drawing from a teacher, playing the bamboo flute and taking pictures.

My hero then was Zhao Chongjia, who was creating a huge sculpture of

Chairman Mao, five to six stories high. I used to work as his assistant, with my Seagull brand 4B 120 double lens camera bought by my parents, I took pictures of the process for creating the sculpture. I used a Seagull brand enlarger to enlarge the pictures.

In 1975, I accompanied my parents from Daqing to the Tianjin Dagang Oilfield, and was assigned to carry out the creation of prints at the district cultural station. When I went to the grassroots to make sketches, I used to take my camera to record materials, and then developed prints in the darkroom of the cultural station. By accident, the publicity department sent me to shoot newsreel and documentary films. I was born to have wide interests, and I devoted myself heart and soul to new things. After I was trained at the Newsreel and Documentary Film Studio, I shouldered a "Gan Guang" 16 cinecamera, and went to the North China Oilfield. In the same year I finished a black-and-white documentary film, which I directed, shot, edited and recorded independently, and it was shown throughout the district. Besides shooting films, I was also responsible for taking still pictures. The unit gave me two cameras; one was a Leica M3 with three lenses, and the other was a Rollei 120 with a double lens. At that time, I mainly took pictures of human figures. I never thought that later I would specialize in landscape photography.

During those years, I shot a large number of black and white negatives and some color negatives. All the color films I used were "Daidaihong" oil-soluble film. I developed and enlarged the pictures myself. I would sometimes stay up in the darkroom all night.

Once Cai Jinhe of the *Workers' Daily* came to the oilfield to conduct interviews. I accompanied him, and he chose several of my photos to depict the workers who "fought Heaven and Earth. " They were published in the *Workers' Daily*. My black-and-white picture titled, "Oilfield Workers in the Snow" was published with comments in the fifth issue of *China Photography* in 1979. This was the first time any of my pictures had appeared in a professional photographic magazine. Maybe that made me lose my enthusiasm for drawing. My teacher, Wang Zhenqi of Harbin Normal University, wrote to me and criticized me for that. Although I felt a little regretful later, I went to work as a department secretary in the Printmaking Department of the China Central Academy of Fine Arts, hoping to take up drawing again, it seemed that I couldn't give up photography. Later, I left the Academy, and went to work at the Civil Aviation Administration of China (CAAC) periodicals office.

In fact I chose to work at CAAC because the conditions there were "superior. " My name is Yuntian (in Chinese it means "clouds and sky"), so maybe there is some kind of hint in the unknown world that I should wander the world over all my life. When I worked for *CAAC Magazine* as a reporter, I got the most professional equipment from the beginning, and I had chances to travel everywhere with free air tickets. At that time photography was a quite luxurious occupation. Ordinary photography fans didn't have the chance to own such nice equipment or go anywhere they wanted to go. The temptation was really quite great for me.

In 1989, I received the highest award of China's photography art—the Golden Statue Award—for a group of pictures with the title "Nine Songs. " I like music, literature, movies and drawing, and all these things helped me a great deal with my photography.

One day, the God of the Nine Rivers, He Bo, reached the top of the Kunlun Mountains, the source of the rivers. He Bo played and swam with maidens in the Nine Rivers. This is the description of the god in the *Nine Songs*, written by the ancient poet Qu Yuan. The artistic description of the poet is magnificent, grand, special and surprising, and full of allusions. This inspired me to create the photographs in the series "Nine Songs." Maybe this can be regarded as a connection between two arts.

**Creation requires thinking alone, being willing to stay alone and being fully devoted to creation, so that you can realize the harmony reached by the noble spirit in the natural world filled with life.**

For more than 20 years I traveled to almost every well-known scenic area in China. I have also traveled in remote deserts, many times driving alone with my photographic equipment, simple cooking gear and the CD I love the most. I have had dialogues with mountains and rivers, wandering about and pondering, and written notes on my travels. This is the way I enjoy life's happiness, and the way I get into contact with Nature. Last August (2007), I went to Ali in Tibet again, taking my son and some fellow photographers. I never thought I could create a record for driving more than 10,000 kilometers without any accident at all at the age of 50.

Creation requires thinking by oneself, in solitude and with whole-hearted devotion, thereby one can realize the harmony reached by the noble spirit in the natural world, which is full of life. This is why I like to travel alone and afar. I like to hide, taking pictures while quietly observing and investigating the infinite secrets hidden in Nature.

In July 1983, I went to Hulun Buir for the first time. I was stranded in Ewenke Town, deep in the grassland, for more than a month, because of a flash flood. I had a dozen rolls of film, one Nikon FE and a Mamiya RB67 camera. When I was about to run out of film, I came up with a smart idea. I made two half-shaded film frames of different specifications with silver paper from cigarette packets. When the pictures were developed, they had unique specifications. I assembled pictures made in this way to form the series "Milky Way," which won a prize.

Ewenke had only 50 to 60 households. Most of the time I spent walking, making sketches, reading books and listening to tapes of classical music. Finally, I learned that the roads were clear, and I could leave. I asked the herdsmen if there were villages nearby. They told me if I walked north along the river I could reach Morigele, the summer camp for horse raisers. Morigele, a Mongolian word, means winding, so I concluded that there must be rivers deep in the grassland. I then took some food and walked to the Morigele River, along countryside roads just as Walt Whitman describes in "Song of the Open Road." The "Milky Way" title picture was taken on that long journey. After many years, a friend asked me: "Where did you take that picture? Where was the winding river?" I couldn't give an answer, for it seemed to have become part of my heart's journey, and there was nowhere to find it.

I often think that I am a very lucky person. I can do the job I like, and enjoy my work. After all, the perfect combination of career and hobby cannot be easily found by most people. Traveling alone for thousands of miles, I feel happy taking superb pictures. But compared with what I experienced in the process, such as life and death, the wonders I saw, the good men I met and the sudden enlightenment I gained, the happiness from the process has been much more than that from the result.

I always believe that everything depends on human effort. It is true most of the time that the fun of life and work is created by yourself. If you are a person with many interests, you will be very happy in your life. For so many years, when I traveled alone, I always cooked breakfast myself. I had a small camp stove. I could boil water on it in five minutes. Then I put some instant noodles and a little Sichuan preserved pickle in it, together with a few pieces of sausage, and I could have breakfast ready in three minutes. At the end of the 1980s, when I traveled in the western part of Sichuan and on the Tibet Plateau, I relied on it. Even when I felt cold and hungry, I could still drink hot coffee and delicious hot soup made from soup stock. When I waited for a suitable light in the sky, I could make a cup of coffee to dispel the cold.

It's impossible for life to be always smooth. As long as you are with other people, it's impossible to have no contradiction, no adversity and no unsatisfactory things at all. Originally I was a press photographer, and joy in my work was my whole joy. But I never thought that when I was 44 I would begin my career again. At that time, *CAAC Magazine*, which I became editor-in-chief of later, was taken over by foreign businessmen. Suddenly, I had to hand in the cameras which had accompanied me for so many years. If I wanted to take pictures again, first I had to buy cameras and films with my own money.

I once wrote an article with the title of "F3 Forever", telling a story of myself and my favorite camera. When I became the press photographer of *CAAC Magazine*, I successively used a Nikon FE, F-501 and F3 provided by the magazine. I clearly remember that at the end of the 1980s, when I travelled in western China and the days and nights when I interviewed and took pictures in Tibet, and climbed Mount Everest, during the day I always took the F3 with me. How proud I was! No matter whether I was in a jeep or an airplane, I always held my camera tightly in my arms and was ready at any moment. At night, in desolate small towns or camping in the field, "she" (F3) was always my pillow, as I feared to lose it. The Nikon F3 accompanied me for many years, although the corners of it had bruises here and there, it was still unexpectedly sturdy. I carried it slung over my shoulder casually, no matter whether it was windy and rainy, or extremely cold and snowy weather, it never let me down. Maybe because of my special feeling for this camera, and maybe because I used it to create the "Nine Songs" series, I finally won the 1st Golden Statue Award in 1989. I always regarded "her" as my treasure and treated her whole-heartedly and carefully. Later, the photographic team was dismantled, and I had to hand in all my photographic equipment. I didn't want to hand in the F3, and later I bought it back when the unit sold the equipment for half price. I bought it together with a Mamiya RB67 camera which I had once used. After all, these old cameras accompanied me in memorable times;

they had become part of my life, and I can never be separated from them, even though I had to borrow the money to buy them!

I swore to start again all over again, at the age of 44. I never mentioned that I had been awarded the Golden Statue Award, and had been an editor-in-chief. I concealed my identity and devoted myself to doing business. As long as I could earn money, I could take pictures of every thing, including themes of daily dining equipment, restaurants, industry, agriculture, township enterprises, famous scenic spots, temples, cemeteries, and living and dead persons. As "an experienced photographer", and with my F3 and Mamiya, I repaid all my debts, and bought various world-famous makes of cameras.

The period I mentioned was the so-called "I have nothing at all." It can be regarded as the time I did pioneering work for the first time in my life. If one experiences owning nothing to owning something, the process may be very happy. But it was quite the contrary for me; I owned something at the beginning, but later I had nothing, and I had experienced a great deal of life's ups and downs. I was once so poor that I had no money even to buy film, and at that time the Oriental Pearl Photo Service allowed me to develop pictures for free. I even told others my name was Xue Fu (man in the snow). I dared not use my real name. Fu to me meant a fellow who had to make a living by laboring to satisfy the very basics of life.

But, in all fairness, that period taught me a lot. Maybe because in my mind there is always a romantic ideal, for many years I always travelled alone, and I gradually learned to understand and deal with all kinds of human relations that I had never thought of before.

The Clouds and Sky Photo Image Gallery was set up by myself and several partners who love photography. It is also a gallery of photographic art works. I deeply realized that in the past we regarded ourselves as artists, who would rather live a poor but "gentlemanly" life, eschewing profit. Many famous photographers have created classic works, but they are always short of money, even lacking the basic photographic conditions, and their works haven't entered the market. They now have great influence, and many followers and fans of photographic art are eager to collect their works, and are proud of possessing them. However, for a long time there was no market for such works, so that neither photographers nor collectors could benefit.

Recalling my photography career, I had glorious days, and I also had hard times. Since I can still work, have some appeal, and there are so many friends who love photography and who support and help me, I think that I should do something for society at large. For so many years, I have deeply experienced the hardship and fun of photography. If I could get more photographers acknowledged and accepted by the market, and bring them some actual benefits, they might improve their conditions for taking pictures and be capable and have more motivation to make finer works. What a good thing that would be! I'm not talking about a long time in the future; I am just talking about the present situation. I don't want other photographers to have experiences like I had when I was 44, and I hope that they will never repeat the sad story of me and my old camera. They should have the highest prestige and live a happy life. The new pioneering work will be different from that of before, and will open a new chapter in my life.

### *Lao Yu, a Marvelous Man*

Walking across Beihuqu Bridge in Wangjing, and then turning left, there are some unique buildings—the Brewery International Art Garden. Many art galleries and studios of artists are located there. The Clouds and Sky Photo Image Gallery set up by famous landscape photographer Yu Yuntian is among them. Yu is an artist with great accomplishments in art and photography. The small area of the Gallery at first gives you the impression that it is a very elegant and comfortable place. Its decorations and arrangement are not like those of a typical art gallery, but more like an elegant place for friends to have a party and chat. But if you look carefully at every picture hanging on the wall, you will feel astonished to find that all these works are by the top photographic artists in contemporary China.

For the order of seniority and age, I should call him Mr. Yu, but Yu Yuntian, who is tall and calm, only accepts being called Lao Yu (Old Yu). No matter how famous he is, those who like photography and his works, and like to discuss them or music and movies with him all call him Lao Yu.

Before the Clouds and Sky Photo Image Gallery was set up, I had read Lao Yu's book containing many sketches and photographs taken during his journeys. When I was reading it, I imagined that Lao Yu was an extremely emotional person. When I met him, he told me that he had spent most of his life wandering around the world, and always travelled alone. Now aged over 50, he realizes that what he gained most was not from his photographic works, but the memories of those days, and the transition from restlessness to calmness.

When he was awarded the Bronze Medal at the national photographic exhibition in 1983, he was still a photographic amateur. When he was awarded the 1st Golden Statue Award in 1989, only six years after becoming a professional photographer, he had already established a distinctive personal style.

Everyone has a special reason for determining his professional ideal. Lao Yu talked about his in a very relaxed way: "I liked the photographer in the film the *Bridges of Madison County*, not because of expecting to encounter any love affairs, but because his was a process of searching for the beauty of nature, having dialogues with mountains and rivers or with himself." The purpose behind the founding of the Clouds and Sky Photo Image Gallery was to promote the classics of China's photography masters, build a platform for the display of contemporary photographic works, search for more market opportunities for Chinese photographers, and gradually build a platform for international photographic artistic exchanges. The Gallery was so named because the partners regard the name of Lao Yu as having great market appeal.

During the two-hour interview, Lao Yu received many calls for advice and instructions. When we talked about the market for photographic artworks, Lao Yu was very enthusiastic. On August 19, when the Clouds and Sky Photo Image Gallery opened for business, there were more than 300 guests from the China Photographers Association, local media, and other artistic circles, including contemporary Chinese landscape photographers and collectors who admire the masters.

Lao Yu has not only produced works that can stand the test of time and are praised by professional photographers, he also has valuable opinions on movies. His drawings are widely appreciated and he has a wealth of stories about his travels in many countries. Asked whom he admired most, he said, "The person whom I admire most is my wife. I really appreciate her writing style, and her other artistic talents and accomplishments." With the support of Lao Yu, his wife published a book of letters written by her and her former lover in memory of her long-lost lover. "They are both excellent painters. Today's young people can hardly understand the pure Platonic love in those special years of the national havoc. That kind of love is more meaningful nowadays." In my opinion, this shows in another way that Lao Yu is a marvelous man.

In the past, Lao Yu could conceal his identity to earn money to buy photographic equipment, make a living and raise his family. When he was 44, he began to do pioneering work and fight for his career. He never betrayed the expectations of the people, and continues to act as a pioneer in the Chinese photographic artwork market, which is still not fully mature. Attitude determines everything. An openhearted man is destined for great success. Let's wish Lao Yu all the best!

# Sorrow and Hope in an Apartment

**Time of interview**: July 5, 2007

**Place**: U. B. C Coffee, Huateng Tower, Beijing

Hong Xiaolong, Male, 24, from Beijing, a college graduate majoring in electronic and information engineering technology, doing technical maintenance for a website.

**Having no apartment of my own, I lost my love.**

Last week, my girlfriend broke up with me. I was so upset. Probably I hadn't lost her completely. Maybe some day we two could get back together again. It happened before. Neither could live without the other, so we got back after the break. But I was extremely upset about this break.

We broke up because I haven't got an apartment of my own. She doesn't mind it, but I hate myself. My parents have a two-bedroom apartment, but it is not mine. I wouldn't have it even if they gave it to me. It has too complicated stories attached to it. When I learned about the stories, I made up my mind never to get married and live in that apartment, since I couldn't bear the torture, the torture of troubled conscience. Of course, I understand that my parents had no choice in those days.

You must be confused. It seems I was talking randomly in a dream, just like in a horror movie. I have to start from the beginning. Let me divide the story into two parts, and begin with the part of my girlfriend and me, since it is shorter, and then I'll tell you my family story. I'm afraid, if I start from my family, I'll waste your time in case I should not finish it.

My girlfriend and I really care about each other. In my third year in college, we rented a small cabin nearby the university, and lived there like a couple. We were both the first love of the other. For many days, we came back after school together, and bought some vegetables in the market and some rice from a small restaurant. When we got home, she would wash the vegetables and make dinner while I talked with her. That feeling was really great! We had an old TV I bought from a neighbor called "Little Henan." It cost us 60 yuan. "Little Henan" collected old electrical appliances. He fixed the TV and installed a satellite antenna for us, so we could see the programs of many TV stations. The TV faced our bed, so we often lay in bed, watching plays. You must be laughing at me! Two college students who should bury themselves in books were actually enjoying their days in a shabby cabin with an old TV. Our parents would think that we lacked ambition. But I really felt happy. Many times I thought, "This is my ideal life—no big house, not much money, no going to bars or restaurants, only living an ordinary life with her, eating her homemade dishes. That would be wonderful." I have never fallen in love with anyone else.

I know I am just too ordinary, not talented or skillful. Nowadays, many college graduates can't find a job. Even when they find one, it isn't a good or well-paid one. Our university is not famous. Our major is not popular. But I'm satisfied that I can earn enough to buy food and clothing for myself. Opportunities always come late, or they may never come and keep me waiting until I die an ordinary man. Who knows?

So I felt great being together with her. She had a unique virtue. She would never force me to do anything to satisfy her wishes. She was not like those girls who drive their men to earn money to buy things for them.

As the saying goes, "He who doesn't plan for the future will find trouble at his doorstep." I once asked her, "Have you thought about our future? We can't live in this rented cabin forever. We will graduate, find a job, get married and have a baby. Have you ever thought about that?" She said, "Yes, I have. Don't worry! We'll make it, step by step. We'll have everything." That's why I treasured her and loved her. She gave me no pressure, only joy and happiness. This is the quality I think every good girl should possess.

If only we could have been students forever! But that's only a dream. When we were students we got money from our parents. It was not that much, but you could never "run out of food. " When I had to really depend on myself, I had to worry about money for the first item. When we entered society, reality smashed many things to pieces, including our love and dreams. Maybe we are just two among thousands of young lovers whose love was smashed.

After I graduated, I got a job in a so-called consultanting company. Actually it was trading stocks for clients. To put it simply, we gathered money from those who wanted to trade stocks but were unable to do so because of their limited time and ability, put the money into the stock market, gave returns to the clients and took a cut for the company according to the amount of money the clients invested. Since the more you put into the stock market, the more you could get out, and besides, our boss had insiders in the securities companies, normally we would not lose money. We young lads, several of us, were in charge of watching the general trend of the stock market, and bought or sold according to the boss's orders. My salary was 1,200 yuan per month, with a free lunch every day. My girlfriend found a job in a company selling baby commodities. Her job was to check whether they had in stock the goods ordered from the Internet, and then arrange the delivery of the goods the next day. She got paid 1,000 yuan per month, also with a free lunch every day. Two months ago, I got my present job, doing technical maintenance for this website. I switch between day shift and night shift every day. My salary is 3,500 yuan a month. She is still with the same company. It's not that easy for girls to change jobs. Besides, she is not very pretty, so she has not as many opportunities as beautiful girls have.

I lived a carefree life in college, knowing nothing about the hardships of life. Now I realize, in less than two years, since I graduated, all my sorrow, regret, shame and hope are closely related to AN APARTMENT.

When we graduated from college, we moved out of the cabin we rented and gave all the things there to "Little Henan. " We said to him "Drop by our apartment" as if we had a new apartment waiting for us to move into. Every time I think of that moment and today's life, I say to myself, "How ridiculous we were!" But compared with today, those days were better. At least we two could live together and depend on each other under the same roof. Now, in this practical world, even our love became a burden.

When I broke up with my girlfriend, she cried, saying she missed our days in the cabin. Her words brought tears to my eyes. She asked me, "Xiaolong, why must you buy an apartment? An apartment is too expensive for us. Your parents have one. We can live with them. If you don't like that, we can rent an apartment. Why must you buy one?" I said, "I must buy my own apartment. My wife and my child should never live with my parents, or in a rented apartment. Without an apartment of my own, I'll never get married." She protested, "Your mum and dad told me they would like to have us in their apartment. Isn't that wonderful?" I said, "No, absolutely not. I can't get married until I get an apartment of my own. You can go if you can't wait. Marry any guy you like." She cried bitterly, saying she couldn't understand how I could change so much, and that she never thought I cared so much about an apartment. When she said this, I thought I was not honest enough with her.

I wonder if there is any man one hundred percent honest with his woman. A man always has something he would not like his wife to know. I once asked my best friend, and he said, "A man has his own reasons. Sometimes he is afraid his woman might be worried or scared, or the woman might meddle in it, or she might look down upon him. Anyway, he can't be so frank and honest. " He asked me what I was afraid of. I couldn't answer him. After a long time, I said I was afraid she would look down upon my parents.

**Grandma never forgave my dad for the rest of her life.**

Speaking of this, I'm a little worried. Will you despise my parents? Will your readers?

To tell you the truth, I myself have despised them since I learned what they did to my grandma, although they were also wretched. I've been suffering from this for half a year, but I kept it a secret. The breakup with my girlfriend made my feelings burst out. In fact, that is why I changed my job and am struggling to make more money.

More than half a year ago, my grandma passed away. My parents didn't go to the funeral. Only I went to bid farewell to her. My father is the only child of my grandma, and in this world only my father and I carry my grandma's blood.

I'm now 24. My parents have been married for 26 years. In those years, my parents and my grandma never called on each other. But Grandma liked me. I went to the kindergarten at the age of four. The kindergarten was in the housing estate my home was in. When we were playing in the housing estate in the morning at 10 o'clock or in the afternoon after our nap, Grandma would come to see me, waving at me in the distance. She knew Grandma Li, the gatekeeper, and it was Grandma Li who told me, "Your grandma is coming to see you. " Did she see me before I was four? I can't remember. I liked this old lady. She bought me food and put me on her knees. Later, we would go back to the classroom to have fruit. Reluctantly she put me down and said she would come back later in a few days. She said with a mysterious expression, "Don't tell Dad Grandma came to see you. " I didn't. I liked her. If I told dad, she would not come; then who would buy candies for me? I kept the secret for many days, until they found it. And I almost got a beating.

It happened when I was in the top class of kindergarten, and only a few days away from primary school. Grandma came about once a month. She left sweets and snacks for me in Grandma Li's place, and Grandma Li gave me some every day. Grandma Li told me that my grandma came every month the day after she got her salary. Once she bought me 500 grams of loose chocolates, and I took a handful from Grandma Li and put them in my pocket. That evening, my mum found them when she took off my pants. She asked where I got them, but I refused to tell her. She was going to beat me, called my dad and said to him that I had stolen money to buy sweets. Extremely irritated, I said, "Grandma bought them for me. " I can't remember more. Little kids are always forgetful. They remember clearly what they eat, but forget bitter experiences. What I'm now telling you is maybe what I later made up when I got to know the truth. I remember my parents, especially my dad, were very angry. It seemed my mum didn't dare to say anything, but just looked at my dad, not knowing how to deal with me and my chocolates. Dad was more experienced. He didn't beat me, but took my hands, and asked me when Grandma first came, what she bought for me, when she usually came and how she was dressed, and so on. I was so encouraged that I couldn't stop talking, and told him everything I knew or I could imagine. I knew he wouldn't beat me if I pleased him, and I felt he was eager to know all that. I described my grandma as a very good old lady, clean, good-looking and hearty, rich and generous, kind and gracious. I used every good word I knew. After I finished, Dad asked Mum to take me to bed, saying nothing more.

Until now my deepest impression about this matter was that later I asked Mum: "Isn't Grandma Dad's mum? Why didn't she come to see Dad? Why didn't Dad go to see her? Why didn't she let me tell Dad she had come to see me?" Mum's answer was vague. She said Grandma was no longer a member of our family. She had married another old man who didn't belong to our family. Since his surname was not Hong, he was not the father of my dad, that is, not

76 The Chinese Dream——
*Real-Life Stories of the Common People in Contemporary China*

my grandpa. My dad was angry with my grandma over this, and they stopped speaking to each other. I was not sure I understood, but who cared? Grandma liked me. That was enough. I didn't care whether my grandpa's surname was Hong or not.

Now I really think my father was too ungrateful, especially when I knew what he had done to my grandma before he got married. He's not a good example for me. Someday when I become a dad, I'll never follow his example. He didn't prevent me from seeing Grandma after he knew she saw me every month. Later, I went to primary school, and then junior high school, both still near my home. Grandma's home was also not far away. She retired before I went to school, but she still came every month. Every time she got her pension, she would come with something she had bought for me, and give me some pocket money. Dad counted the days. Many times when he thought Grandma was coming, he told me: "Xiaolong, ask Grandma to buy you a pair of gym shoes," or something else. They shifted their duty onto Grandma, and let her pay for many things that were not the least trivial. At first, I told Grandma whatever Dad told me to say. I said Dad had asked her to buy a pair of gym shoes for me. Grandma agreed, and waited until school was over to take me to buy a pair. Things like this happened almost every month, and Grandma never let me down. She bought everything I asked for. But I didn't think it was right for Dad to do that, and found it embarrassing to ask Grandma for anything. Once Dad said, "Ask your grandma to buy you a down jacket." I said, "Why don't you buy me one?" He said, "Grandma likes you, doesn't she? Besides, she has a lot of money. On whom can she spend her money except on you?" I said, "Am I not your son? It's a dad's duty to raise his son. You can't ask others to pay what you should pay for me." Do you think I then "had independent thoughts"? I'm not sure. But I always thought Grandma was taken advantage of by my parents.

When I entered senior high school, Grandma began to visit me less. Every time she came, she gave me several hundred yuan, but didn't let me spend the money. She took me to the nearby Construction Bank, deposited it into an account in my name, saying, "Xiaolong, keep it for college."

I once asked Grandma why she didn't call on my parents. She said they were busy and she didn't like to bother them. I thought a kid could say whatever he wanted, so I told her what Mum had said about her, and asked whether she was ashamed to visit us as she was no longer a member of the Hong family. Grandma said nothing, but she looked as if she were going to cry. I'm not a considerate person; in fact, I'm selfish. As long as others treat me well, I care about nothing. But in fact I knew what was right and wrong, and felt that my dad was not a filial son, for he never asked about Grandma's health or what she needed or how she lived. The only thing he did was to tell me to ask Grandma for money.

I once saw Grandma's "eldest son," that is, the eldest son of the old man she later married. That old man had three sons and two daughters. He himself was a doctor of traditional Chinese medicine, a few years older than Grandma. Grandma was so unfortunate to have my dad, but she was lucky to marry that old man. His children treated her very well, much better than my dad did. I remember once at the school gate, I was walking my bicycle with Grandma when a black Audi stopped near us. Out of the car stepped a man older than my dad. Grandma stopped. The man called her "Mum," and Grandma seemed a little embarrassed. She turned to me, and told me to call the man "uncle," saying that he was her "eldest son." He patted me on the shoulder, saying "You are Xiaolong? Come by with Grandma sometime." Then he asked Grandma: "Mum, are you going home?" Grandma said yes. So he said, "Then I'll give you a lift." But Grandma insisted on going with me, saying she wanted to talk to me. Then he drove away, waving goodbye to me. That moment I had a strange feeling I couldn't describe. I sensed this man was not the same type as my parents. People like to use the word "class." He apparently didn't belong to the same "class" as my parents. I didn't know why I had the feeling that he was more decent than my dad. If I had had the choice, I would have chosen to be like him, rather than like my dad. I liked his manner better. Don't laugh at me. I really think so, and I never liked my dad, let alone admired him.

When I entered college, Grandma was very happy, and decided to take me out to a good dinner. She was very old then. I had an idea of putting her in contact with my parents. I thought no matter how much they misunderstood each other, with so many years going by and everyone getting old, they could have a talk then. I thought it was no big deal, only that my dad hadn't agreed to Grandma remarrying, and thought she had brought shame on the family. It was very common for people to be against their mother's second marriage at that time. My grandma was so modern!

But Grandma didn't agree, saying that I was only a kid and should not get involved in grown-ups' business. My dad also said, "It's none of your business." Later, he said, "Even if I wanted to see her, she wouldn't want to see me. She has three sons now, and she doesn't need me!"

Grandma was never reconciled with my dad for the rest of her life. Later, I got to know that it was because she was totally heartbroken. I guess at her last moment, she might have been very sad, for those around her deathbed were not her own children, while her real son was selfish and ungrateful.

## My dad arranged for Grandma to remarry to get the apartment.

I learned everything from the "eldest son." He was almost 60 then. Grandma died of a heart attack in Beijing Union Medical College Hospital. The "eldest son" informed me of her heart attack immediately, but when I got to the hospital she had passed away. The five children of their family, with all their children, were there. The "eldest son" drew me aside, and said, "Xiaolong, please understand. We respect her wish not to call your father." With mixed feelings, I couldn't say anything, but just wept. I guess Grandma had already planned for that day, and she had decided never to give my parents a chance to be forgiven and she wouldn't let them bid her farewell. What bitter hatred could make a mother and her own son become enemies unable to be reconciled even on her deathbed? I really wondered.

It was the "eldest son" who told me everything after Grandma was cremated. It was a serious man-to-man talk. I even feel that I grew up because of that talk. It was on the side of the street near Babaoshan cemetery, in his car. He told the driver to take a walk, and he would call him if he needed him. Then he sat in the driver's seat, with me beside him. He gave me a cigarette, and said, "Xiaolong, you are a good boy. You want to know what happened between your father and your grandma? Now Grandma has gone, and I'm going to tell you. This is what your grandma asked me to tell you. She hoped you can be a filial and independent man. "

What I'm going to tell you is just what I heard from him. I'll try to tell you exactly what he told me.

My grandfather died very early, and Grandma brought up my father. As a worker in a clothes factory, my grandma couldn't earn much. My grandfather didn't leave anything, but when he died the enterprise he worked for offered my dad a chance to work there, and also changed the three-room bungalow they gave our family into an apartment with two bedrooms. My dad later built up a good relationship with the leaders of the enterprise, and became a driver for them. But some years later, their enterprise went bankrupt, so he was forced to retire.

The "eldest son" said he was told this after his father died. He said my grandma was very kind, honest and industrious, and they considered her their own mother. They were really grateful for my grandma's attendance on their father so that their father could live a happy life in his old age. His father's will was to leave half of his savings to my grandma and give each child one-fifth of the other half. As long as my grandma lived, his apartment belonged to her. When she died, his children could sell it and distribute the money among themselves. Among the five children, four are college graduates. They were all well off, and had their own apartments. No one cared about their father's three-bedroom apartment. Then their father died, leaving my grandma alone. One day she called the "eldest son" to their home. She was very upset, weeping, and telling him she didn't want to stay there any more, since their father had died and she didn't like to bother his children. She asked them to sell the apartment, and share the money. As for herself, she would go to a rest home for the elderly. The "eldest son" said, "No, we can't let you go to a rest home. Although our father has died, you are still our mother. We will perform our filial duties to you. We don't think a rest home is a bad place but it is our shame to send you there." Then my grandma told him how she married his father.

It was just before my parents got married that my grandma became their stepmother. My mum often went to our home then. Every time she came, my dad would ask Grandma to "go for a walk" in advance. He also made a signal for Grandma. Since the kitchen window was facing the outside street, my dad would put a vegetable basket on the windowsill when my mum was leaving. Seeing the basket, Grandma would know she could come back home. I couldn't understand why Dad did this. It was said that he thought that with my grandma at home they would not feel "easy." Weren't there two bedrooms? Why should they drive Grandma out? I still feel that my father is a typical selfish man. When the "eldest son" told me the shameful things my dad did, he didn't comment or use any scornful or reproachful words. But I was so uneasy in his car, for I knew he despised my parents, although he didn't say anything.

Grandma never complained about this. Later, Mum came more often. In the cold winter, Mum and Dad watched TV in Grandma's bedroom, and closed the door of the smaller bedroom, which was my father's, while Grandma had to "walk" outside. They never cared that my old grandma was cold. Once my grandma could not see the basket on the windowsill, but she had to use the toilet. When she came back, she found nobody at home. Dad had forgotten their signal, and kept Grandma waiting in the cold outside.

My parents were preparing for their marriage. Without conferring with Grandma, my dad asked a group of his friends to make the balcony a closed room. The balcony was in Grandma's room. Dad said, it was good to make the balcony another room, so that Grandma could move there and her big bedroom could be turned into a living room. Thus my grandma had to sleep on the balcony. It was cold in winter, since there was no central heating. When summer came, it was so hot that Grandma had to leave the window open all day, and her bed became covered with dust. My dad didn't care, as if it had nothing to do with him.

Later my dad asked Grandma to clear away her things and "throw those useless things out to save room. " Thus Grandma had to sell some of her clothes, shoes and many old things she had treasured for a long time.

My grandma said to the "eldest son" that my mum had seen all this. Grandma was not sure whether it was their decision not to keep her in their home. She could only scold her son in her heart for being so unfilial.

But this was not the worst thing. What made her most heartbroken was that my dad was asking others to find a husband for Grandma. He was arranging for his old mother's second marriage! This second husband was the father of the "eldest son. "

The "eldest son" said that he had heard some of my grandma's story from the neighbors. You remember the gatekeeper of my kindergarten, Grandma Li? Her husband was an old friend of the father of the "eldest son. " My dad had the nerve to ask Grandma Li to help find someone suitable for Grandma. He said Grandma was not that old, so it was better for her to have a husband than live with her son and daughter-in-law. Grandma Li told my grandma that her son was not to be relied on, so it would be better for her to find another husband. And so my grandma met the father of the "eldest son. " His family was well off. The old man was a doctor of traditional Chinese medicine, and could make a lot of money. The old man had his own apartment, and his children always gave him money. The children wanted to find their father a wife of about his own age to take care of him, for they thought a wife would be closer than his children.

My grandma said she was heartbroken. She couldn't have imagined that after so many years of widowhood she would be married off by her own son to make room for her daughter-in-law. No one knew how my grandma felt when she moved out of her home. She only took with her some clothes. When my dad found out that Grandma had found a suitor, he said, "Get married then, before my wedding. Otherwise how could a daughter-in-law arrange the marriage of her mother-in-law shortly after her own wedding?" So Grandma got married before the wedding of my parents.

My grandma went to the apartment when my dad got married. It was interesting that the apartment belonged only to the young couple, without any room for the mother. I guess my dad dared not tell others he had had to marry his widowed mother off to an old man before he could marry his wife.

That is why Grandma never saw my parents after that. She said that when she remarried she told my dad that his wedding would be the last time they would meet.

Can you imagine how I felt in that luxurious car, listening to the mean things my dad had done to my grandma? I was so uneasy. To be fair, my grandma was lucky to marry their father. If she hadn't been able to find a good husband when she was driven out by her own son I might have lost her many years ago.

## Grandma's ashes will be with me wherever I go.

From that time on, I hated to go home, especially to see my dad. He didn't know Grandma had died, since I didn't tell him. I wondered when he, her son, could have a moment to think about his own mother. Finally he thought of her, because of her apartment.

My girlfriend came to my home sometimes after I got a job. My parents approved of our relationship. Once we were having dinner together, and Mum said a neighbor had had a baby. "When can I become a grandma?" she asked. I hated to listen to her talking like that. I was sensitive about this matter, since I was thinking of my grandma. I had been born in that apartment, and had a room of my own. It seemed we were a perfect family. But what was the cost? My grandma had to remarry at such an advanced age. Even though she was well treated, she had to attend upon another family. It made me sad whenever I thought of it. My girlfriend went away after dinner once, and Dad was cleaning the table. Mum said, "She has to come and go like that. How tiring! Why don't you two get married? You can live in the big room, and your dad and I can sleep in the small room. When you have enough money to buy a big apartment you can move out, and we can stay here and look after your child." Mum liked gabbing, so I kept silent. Suddenly Dad said, "Your grandma has an apartment. Her husband is dead. I don't know whether it has passed to her or not." I was furious. "You forced Grandma to remarry," I shouted. "Now you've got your greedy eyes on her apartment!" Mum and Dad were shocked. Dad rushed at me, threatening to kill me. Mum dragged him back, crying and shouting to me to run away.

I ran outside. I was drinking beer and eating shish kebab all alone until midnight. When I went back home, they were waiting for me. Mum had swollen eyelids and Dad had long face. But he couldn't beat me. I know, he's mean, but he truly loves me. Mum let me sit down, and then Dad asked, "How did you know all that?" I said, "It's none of your business. I know it." He said, "You don't know." I said, "It's no use. My grandma is dead."

It was the first time I saw Dad with tears in his eyes. He asked, his voice trembling, "When did she?"

"Almost two months ago. She's been cremated. "

"When did you see her last?"

"When I saw her last she had passed away. "

Then he was silent, hanging his head, sitting on the sofa. I didn't like to see him like that. For a moment I pitied him. But it was too late for regrets. For a moment I thought he deserved it.

I had a sleepless night. Several times I heard Mum ask Dad to sleep, but he said, "Leave me alone. "

I remember the "eldest son" said to me that day, "Xiaolong, I think you have grown up. These grudges belong only to the older generation. Don't be troubled. Find a proper time to talk with your parents and discuss how to deal with your grandma's ashes. We agree if you wish to bury her with your grandfather. Otherwise, we'll find a good day to bury her ashes with my father and mother. " Grandma hadn't made a will. Perhaps she didn't know how to make one about this matter. She hated her own son, and never forgave him. She might never want to go back to our Hong family. But she was not the first wife of her second husband. Did she belong in their tomb? Every time I think of this I can't help crying. Grandma was really such a pathetic woman. She couldn't decide her own fate when she was alive, nor could she decide about her ashes.

Several times I wanted to say to Dad: "let's bury Grandma with Grandpa. She's not inferior to others. She also has a son and a grandson. " But I didn't. I couldn't.

Since the fight with Dad, I have hardly spoken to him. I felt terrible so I decided to rearrange my life. The first thing I did was to change my job. I didn't care too much about money before, but now I'm going to try to find every possible way to make more money. I'll buy my own apartment. I have no doubt my parents love me, and even if they hurt the whole world, they won't hurt me. I clearly remember they said to me: "Xiaolong, we don't have much money, so we can't buy you an apartment when you get married. But don't worry. You can stay here. " But I'll manage to have a good life by myself, rather than by taking advantage of my parents. The second thing I did was to find the "eldest son," and tell him that I had decided to split in half my grandma's ashes. Half of her ashes will be theirs, for she was their stepmother. I'll keep the other half, and take her with me wherever I go.

Now you can understand why I'm so determined to buy an apartment. It is now my greatest wish, although I lost my girlfriend for it.

## Interviewer's Notes

### Can We Find Happiness Without Our Own Apartment?

When I was waiting for Hong Xiaolong at the gate of U. B. C coffee this morning, cars were slowly pulling into the parking lot. I counted the number, and calculated their prices. A BMW530, may cost 600,000 yuan? A Honda Fiat Saloon, 100,000 yuan should be enough. Then Hong's joke came into my mind. When he heard of our meeting place, he said "I'm scared of seeing tall buildings and luxury cars." And I said, "Then that's your bad luck. Tall buildings and luxury cars are everywhere in Beijing."

Hong Xiaolong came on time. White T-shirt, jeans, NIKE sneakers and no socks, a youthful face. He was carrying a square, black bag (I could see it was a laptop). "I've just come off night shift." He said, shyly.

We found a place in the back corner of the cafe. I asked if he had had dinner. He said he wasn't hungry, and just wanted a drink of water. I ordered an iced "blue mountain" coffee, but he said at once "No. I'm not drinking that. I only need water, just water with ice." He was speaking with gestures, eager to let the waitress know. The pretty waitress gave him a cold stare and went away with a "one minute." "She's not happy about the price?" curiously he asked me, with a naughty smile. I said, "Water is so cheap. So I ordered a not-so-cheap coffee, otherwise they would come many times, asking what you need or cleaning the table, to show their dislike." He guffawed, "Really! I thought you liked it. To me, all kinds of coffee are the same, tasting like instant herbal mixture for curing a cold. Next time, just order plain water, and see if they drive you out."

I didn't answer. I knew that that was where we were different from each other—I and the 24-year-old Hong Xiaolong. I would prefer to pay for a moment of peace, so I won't order a cheap drink, just to avoid being interrupted by the waitresses. But he would insist—I'm your customer and I have the right to order anything I like.

Before we decided to meet, I asked Hong Xiaolong to summarize his story in one sentence. He thought for a moment, and said, "I'd like to tell you from my own experience how important an apartment is to an ordinary Chinese person." Following this summary, Hong Xiaolong told me the story of him, his parents, his grandma and the apartment. What he was most concerned about was what I thought of his father and what his father had done to his grandma. Several times he asked me, "Do you look down upon my parents?" I said, no. He was not quite convinced. "Why don't you? You just don't want to hurt me, do you?" I said, no. I understood them. Besides, I'm not sure whether I could have done better if I had been in their shoes. So I don't feel I have the right to look down upon them.

In the same parking lot where we met, cars were coming and going. We said goodbye to each other, and then he walked south. Gazing at him walking away, I felt sad, for I remembered that he had told me that on the top of his bookcase was a box containing half of his grandma's ashes.

That evening I wrote a letter to Hong Xiaolong at his request to know my true opinion about his story:

July 5, 2007

Dear Xiaolong,

Thank you for your trust, and for introducing me to the life of the three generations in your family. However, I felt that you still couldn't believe in me completely. You don't believe I don't look down upon your parents. I would like to tell you it is true. And I think your doubt of me is because you are confused, and you don't know how to judge properly. Maybe when you are my age you will understand that many things in life are neither right nor wrong. Let's try to understand life slowly.

Your story is stimulating for people of my age. Almost all ordinary people over 30, living in cities, without any special professional or good family background, more or less have some unpleasant memory about apartments, no matter whether they have their own or not. The three generations of your family number among thousands and thousands of such families. The memories of apartments with all the bitterness and warmth are special in this era and in China.

I'd like to tell you two stories about apartments, and both are true.

The first story is about a couple and their son. The couple is younger than 60 years old now, but last year they moved with their pension into a rest home for the elderly in Changping District. They are the youngest among those in the rest home. Their one-bedroom apartment was given to their only son, who has a son of his own now. They were not driven out by their son, but moved out voluntarily. They said to their old neighbors and friends that life in the rest home was better, and they didn't need to wash clothes or cook. I don't know if they were telling the truth, but I know what happened before they moved. When he was 22, the son took his girlfriend home. In less than two years, he said, he wanted to marry her. How could the parents live together with the young couple in such a small apartment with only one bedroom? The old couple racked their brains, and finally got an idea. They removed the wall separating the balcony and the bedroom, and then divided the larger "room" into two rooms. The son agreed, but the young couple wanted the room closer to the living room and bathroom. When they started to live like this, the old couple realized how "inconvenient" it was, like living on top of one another. Soon the daughter-in-law decided to get a divorce, saying she could no longer bear that life with "no privacy." Their son wept: "What can I do, Mum and Dad?" Can you imagine how they felt at that moment? How many heartbreaking, embarrassing details were there in their life? You can just imagine, as many as you like. I'll only tell you the end: The old couple left while their son was redecorating their apartment. He was reunited with his wife, and is said to be living a happy life.

The second story is about a couple and their daughter living in a cabin of less than 15 square meters. The couple could enjoy their own room only after the daughter went to college. I once visited their home. All the furniture is simple, and made by the husband. Since they need to make full use of the limited space, they have to make their own furniture. From every piece of furniture you can see his wisdom and thought. Under the double bed are a single bed and a desk. On the other side of the stairs from the double bed is a little cupboard. Beside the wardrobe of the daughter, you find a cabinet. Next to the cabinet, there is a TV stand and a foldaway dining table. They have special wallpaper, which is in fact pieces of colored cloth sewn together, hanging down from the roof and covering the wall. On the "wallpaper" there are various kinds of little pockets containing articles for daily use, such as medicine, needles and thread, and cosmetics. The wife told me the cabin was so damp that sometimes the walls exuded water. So they pasted thick and hard plastic cloth on the walls and roof. Then they decided to hide the ugly plastic cloth with some colorful cloth, and unexpectedly they found themselves with special wallpaper. They are not rich, but they are enjoying a life that cannot be bought.

From the first story, you can see that life can be hard without an apartment; the quality of life can be influenced if one has no apartment of one's own. From the second story, you can also see those who have no apartment or much money are not necessarily unhappy. Happiness in life is in fact not necessarily connected with money.

Therefore I really hope you can strive hard to make more money, to realize your dream and totally change your life. I also hope you can learn to create and find the joy of life in everyday living, while your dream is still some distance away. Rome was not built in a day, but every day you can be happy.

I hope your dream will come true soon!

An Dun

# Atonement on the Premise of Love

**Time of interview**: May 2, 2008

**Place**: Beijing Kerry Center

Jin Yu, male, 48, from Beijing. After graduation from college, he worked in a government office until he went into business in 1994. Since then, he has established two cultural communication companies and an advertising company. In 2006 he returned to school for an EMBA diploma, and is now a professional manager.

**When her father asked whether she would like to marry me because of my wealth, she felt curious. She asked: "Is that a reason for marriage?"**

I hung around your blog. On the notice-board you said you wanted to meet someone with great ideals, miracles, rich experiences and thoughts—symbols of the present-day Chinese spirit. You know what I thought when I saw that? I thought it was too high a standard for ordinary Chinese people. What kind of dreams of those small potatoes can be counted as your so-called Chinese Dreams?

Take me and the people around me, for example. Probably we never have a dream about the nation, but each of us has a dream of our own. It's a dream close to our living conditions and a dream of changing our present situation. If realized, it means we've reached the lifestyle we want most within the shortest time. Then we can be happy and joyful, and can devote ourselves to social construction without any mental burden, fearing no bitterness or tiredness, or anything. We are willing to do all this to feel mentally comfortable. I'm not being garrulous. I'm telling the truth. All dreams of harvest and happy life of the small potatoes, I think, make a bigger dream of Chinese struggling for happiness. What do you say? No individuals, no collective.

So I decided to tell you the story of my sorrows and happiness. I've repeated many times in my heart what I want to tell you. I'm thinking of it every day. I want the woman I'm pursuing to know what I'm thinking.

The woman I'm pursuing is my ex-wife. She's the woman I love most and whom I failed most.

If I still have a life dream, that's to go back to her and live the rest of my life with her, no matter what condition she is in. I remember hearing the fairy tale *The Fisherman and the Golden Fish*. When caught, the golden fish told the old fisherman: "Grandpa, if you free me, I'll satisfy all your requirements." I really hope I can meet such an almighty golden fish, and ask it to satisfy my dream, so that my life will be perfect.

Let me talk about my ex-wife.

I met her at the age of 34. She was ten years younger than I and had been out of college for two years. At the time I had a son whose mother had left and married a man much older than she. The man was richer than I. Maybe she decided she loved money better than me. She thought even if I could become the head of a government office my economic prospects would still not be bright. So she left. I kept the child, as she had hoped. She didn't want to take him for that would make it hard for her to remarry. My ex-wife is my second wife. My first divorce finally forced me to give up my government job and establish a small company with a few friends. By 1994, we had already made some achievements in trade.

And then I met her.

It was a coincidence. I remember it was an April morning, a book store in a small street park near my house was having a promotion. We both took a fancy to a book at the same time. When I was about to pay after browsing it, she picked it up. "I'm buying it," I said. "Oh, what a pity," she said. I didn't see her face but I heard her voice—very gentle it was—which made me curious about its owner. Then I saw her in a scarlet suit, a short skirt and red high-heeled shoes, like a bride. She returned the book to me, and then a special feeling came into my heart. Afterwards I thought maybe my instinct had told me at that time that the book would be our common wealth one day so I would like to let her take it. I paid for it when she had already gone to the other side of the stall. I followed her, and said: "If you really like it you can read it, but remember to return it to me." She stared at me with a smile on her face as if I was not a stranger to her.

We agreed to meet in the small park three days later, and she would return the book.

She was working as a translator in a foreign company at that time, but she was in fact her boss's secretary.

She was very pure and cheerful, lacking love experience, but with good family courtesy education, which I had realized when we had just begun our relationship. One thing very important about her was that she had little money concept, which a divorced person like me would attach great importance to. I didn't want a woman who always chased money any more. Here are two examples: Once we ate at Pizza Hut. She liked two kinds of pizza with different flavors, and couldn't make her mind up. I ordered both, and something else. There were at last two half-pancakes left over. "May I pack them? I can take them to the office tomorrow," she asked. Maybe due to vanity, I told her I could buy her fresh ones if she liked. "Oh, no," she said, "We can't waste such tasty food." Another time we went to Scitech to buy clothes. It was a very expensive shop at that time. "Choose what you like," I told her. After looking around carefully, she bought a blouse worth about 200 yuan. "Too ordinary," I said, and recommended a one-piece dress worth more than 4,000 yuan. She loved it, but when she saw the price she dragged me away, and whispered, "It's not for sale. It's for exhibition. Too dear to wear." I was determined to marry her then.

After overcoming many difficulties, we got married. It was hard to convince her parents, for after all I was many years older than she was and I had a child. Her parents didn't accept me for a long time. Then she told me once her dad had asked her whether she wanted to marry me because of my wealth. She asked, "Is that a reason for marriage?" In fact, I didn't have much money. My living standard was just above average. When we were in love she didn't know clearly what I was doing for a living. Even after marriage she still asked me: "What do you sell?"

She treated me and my son very well, beyond my expectation. At that time I only hoped they could get along well. My son lived with my parents, and only came to stay with us at weekends. I was worried that they would refuse to accept each other, but I was wrong. My son had a closer relationship with her than with me. They were like partners. Then the two-day weekends began, and on Friday they would contact each other to decide their activities at the weekend. She would go to my parents' to pick up my son, even when I was out on business. So when we got divorced, my son felt very regretful because he had lost a person who loved him and a friend.

**I betrayed my family and love. I wanted to take revenge for her restrictions on me. I couldn't stand her neurotic torment, and wanted a mature woman to take care of and comfort me.**

Our bad relationship began in the sixth year of our marriage. At that time I had already left the original company, and established my own, and she got another job as a full-time translator, often working at home. I was busy being in charge of the company. I had to attend many social occasions, and so paid less and less attention to her. On the other hand, she paid more and more attention to me; maybe it was because she had no life pressure and too much leisure, and had become very willful owing to my indulgence. But I was selfish about one thing—I didn't want to have another child, for I thought one son was troublesome enough and one more child would exhaust us. But a long time after that I understood I was wrong for I was depriving her of being a mother, and putting her into a state of loneliness and giving her a sense of loss. But at that time I just didn't understand, which is a pity.

Maybe because she was lonely, she was always worried about me. I went out early and came back late, leaving her at home alone facing novels to be translated or foreign books, and a pile of reference books. What's more, she wasn't good at taking care of herself. I was the cook in our family, and I arranged everything. She was used to buying vegetables, chopping them up and waiting for me to cook them. I drove her anywhere she wanted to go, we watched DVDs and TV, and read books together in the evening, and I escorted her back to her parents'. But suddenly these were all gone, and she kept bothering me with the excuse that I ignored her and was loving her less and less. At last she was kind of neurotic, and accused me of having an affair.

I tried helping her. I gave her money and let her go to a beauty salon. But she refused, for she said she wasn't in the mood and nobody wanted to see her beauty, and her husband just wanted to see other beauties. I offered to buy her a car, and let her go where she wanted to, but she said, "No. I'm used to being a passenger. And if I die in an accident, another woman will replace me. " I urged her to go back to school and get a diploma in her favorite subject, but she said she was literate enough, and if she had been an illiterate housewife she wouldn't have been so annoyed. She would phone me all the time, beginning with "Where are you?" She forced me to tell her where I was and what I was doing whatever time or occasion it was or whatever I was busy with. If I failed to do that, she would be angry and quarrel with me when I got home. I was annoyed, and she was annoyed for she cared about me and our marriage. I just didn't understand. What I knew was she was different, boringly different, and what I did was to blame her blindly.

Neither of us was happy in that situation, and that was a perfect time for a third person to appear. Unluckily, I met another woman. She was in the same industry as I was, and had been divorced. She was three years older than my wife, and looked very mature. At first we just had some business relations. When we were talking business sometimes my wife would call, which made me feel embarrassed. After a while, the woman asked whether I was having problems with my wife. Did she lack trust in me. "Yes. " I said, "I can't help it. My wife is younger than I. She has nothing to do every day and takes tracing me as her job. " She sympathized with me, and so I found we had something in common. Our relationship became closer and closer. Then she asked to become a partner in my company. My wife warned me against her. I just ignored her. But, in fact, she was right. This was proven at a very high cost afterwards.

I went to Changsha on business. My wife kept calling me, so I had turned off my cell phone. That night, I drank too much, and at last I slept with that woman. The next morning, I thought, "She keeps saying I am having an affair, and now it's really happening. " But I couldn't stand her neurotic torment; I wanted a mature woman to take care of and comfort me.

**I deserved it. I hurt my ex-wife, and I deserved being dumped.**

Back in Beijing, that woman and I became an immoral couple, as defined by my wife when we divorced: "Jin Yu, I really judged you wrongly. I thought a gentleman like you would have any divorce excuse except for an affair. I didn't expect you would be so shameful. " She was right. I was very shameful, for I hurt my wife for another woman.

Objectively I was taking this affair very seriously, for she was good at taking care of people in both life and spirit. She made me relax, whereas my ex-wife had been able to do nothing but try to control me. Now I want to tell all men following in my footsteps: When your love becomes your wife she might be worse than your original wife. But at the time I just felt my love was good, and sometimes I even thought it was wrong for me to have married such an innocent girl; I should have married a mature woman so that I could have fun in both spirit and life. I was being stupid. I thought that that woman was the one with whom I could spend the rest of my life. On the other hand I thought my wife too annoying. She said she loved me, but her love was a spiritual burden to me; though my love never said she loved me, she was able to make me comfortable without any conditions. I have something else to say: Don't think your love will give you unselfish and pure love without conditions, because when she becomes your wife one day she would have more conditions and requirements. Moreover, her love is definitely not pure, for she comes from nowhere and is good at scheming.

The most ridiculous thing was that I bought that woman a flat, where I wanted to spend the rest of my life with her. Absurd! When we signed a contract in the sales office, she said, "Sign your name. That way, even if you change your mind you wouldn't suffer a great loss. Anyway, you are what I want, though I don't know what is in your mind. " Then I held her in my arms and gave her the flat. It turned out that she was the first to change her mind. She met a man who said he would take her to Singapore. She left with most of my money, including one million yuan from the sale of the flat I had given her.

Back to my ex-wife. She was very stubborn. She loved romantic stories and hated injustice. She had no way to prove that I was having an affair, but I wanted a divorce. The more intimate I was with that woman, the less I wanted to go home, and the less I wanted to go home, the more trouble my wife would make. She was really very painful at that time. "Jin Yu, you are having an affair," she once said. "Don't deny it, and don't think I'm insulting you. I'm your wife. I know you well." Sometimes when I went home late at night she would be sitting in the living room and drinking wine. I said to her: "The more you act like this, the more I dislike you. I'm leaving you, not because I'm having an affair but because I can't stand you."

One morning, I left the file concerning the flat I had bought for my mistress on my desk on purpose before I went to work. At about ten in the morning she came to my office, put that file on my desk and said, "Jin Yu, let's get a divorce. I told you when I married you that if I knew you had another woman I wouldn't cling to our marriage one more minute. But now I know everything. It's finished." At the time I felt something sink down in my heart. I didn't know whether it was a light or heavy feeling—a little regretful with a sense of relief. "Go home. Let's talk at home," I answered. At this, she cried, "Jin Yu, from now on I have no home."

In 2001 we divorced. I left our flat, having given some money to her. The money was enough for her to live on for three to five years. Then I began to live with that woman in the other flat. But once we began to live together, conflicts arose between us, for we suddenly realized that we were going to have to face each other every day from then on. One morning I woke up, to see that she was already dressed up. She told me she was going back to her house to clean it, and had entrusted the new flat to a part-time maid. Only at that time did I begin to realize that we both had our own families before, and this flat was just a place for rendezvous. Now I had lost my home, but hers was still there. After she left I asked myself whether I had done the right thing. Very soon I realized that actually I didn't know her well, and her life was much more complicated than my ex-wife's.

In the summer of 2004 we broke up over her affair with the Singapore guy. She sold the flat, and I was left homeless.

I moved to a house I rented. Soon she went abroad. I deserved it. I had hurt my ex-wife, and I deserved to be dumped.

**My ex-wife's life dream was our marriage. But I broke it into pieces.**

Once my single life began, I realized that the one I missed most was my ex-wife. It was then that I realized she had been in love with me without any conditions. Let me put it this way. She never wanted to control my money like so many women do. She was in fact not good at taking care of herself, and she didn't know how to cook. But she always dressed me in tidy and clean clothes, and she even ironed my shirts in person. She hung eight shirts with ties on the clothes rack, with an extra one for emergency use. She polished my shoes, wrapped them in soft cloth, and put them on the shoe rack in good order. She kept our house decorated with flowers in full blossom. Even when we broke up she didn't asked me for any money.

One day I found a set of keys in a drawer. They were the keys to the door of our previous house. I drove back to our house. I opened the door just to find everything was where it had been. All the furniture and the quilts on the bed were still there, and there was still coffee in the coffee maker in the kitchen. It seemed that she was still living there. All sorts of feelings sprang up in my mind. If we hadn't divorced, maybe we would be living in peace now. She still hadn't changed the keys. Didn't she know that I still had a set?

I sat in the living room for a while, but touched nothing. Then I left. From that day on, I began to be curious about her life. I wanted to know how she was, what kind of people she was meeting and how they treated her. Sometimes I even worried whether she could accustom herself to others, for I had indulged her that much. If they took advantage of her, what could she do? At the thought of this I would be very sad.

But I didn't have the courage to call her; I knew she hated me and everything I had done to her.

In the summer of 2007 I ran into one of our old neighbors. She said my wife had moved back with a child and had divorced again. I didn't know how to describe my feelings, but you could say my world broke down.

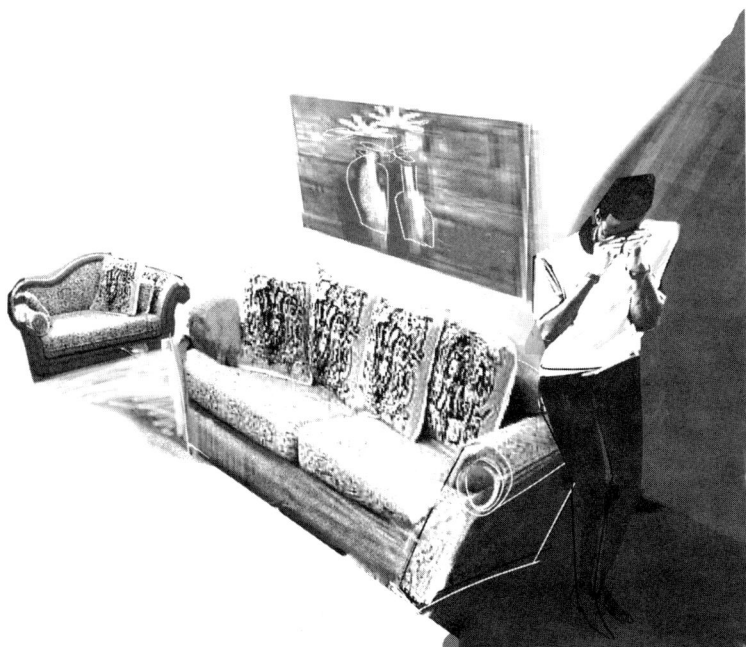

The same afternoon I went back with that set of keys, but they didn't work any more. Then I heard the sound of a key inside. I hurried downstairs, and hid behind the security guard's office. I wanted to see her without being noticed. A little while later she came out with a little girl, about two years old, in a shabby pram. I was very sad that day. My ex-wife is not beautiful, but she used to have a very vivid and lively face, and her skin used to be very smooth. When we broke up, she looked haggard and tough, but not old at all. But now the woman had totally changed. She was already a one-hundred-percent middle-aged woman.

Later that day I drove aimlessly for quite a long time. Finally I parked my car, and called a friend, a lawyer who is a friend to both of us. I thought if she had really got divorced again she must have turned to him for help. My first words were "Is my ex-wife divorced?" The guy was caught by surprise. "You didn't know that? They divorced when their baby was only one year old, and the man got married again and his new wife is pregnant now."

In brief, after our divorce, she lived alone for over half a year, and then met the owner of a printing house. He was a successful businessman, divorced and had no children. But their relationship went from bad to worse after my ex-wife got pregnant, and her husband found out that it was going to be a girl. He tried to get her to have an abortion, but she refused. At last they reached an agreement to divorce after the child was born.

"Did he give her any money" I asked the lawyer. "Yes. " "How much?" "1,000. " "How much does he make?" "At least 20,000 a month, and sometimes more than 100,000. " I was incensed. My lawyer friend was silent for a while, and finally said, "In fact it was all your fault. If you hadn't divorced her she would never have made that mistake. Now she can't make both ends meet with only translation work, because she has a baby. "

After going back home, I couldn't fall asleep, so I began to drink. But it only made me sadder. My brain was teeming with everything that had been between us in those days. At midnight, I woke up my lawyer friend with a phone call. "I want to marry her again and be a father to her baby. " I said. "If you have made up your mind, go chase her. She is still in love with you, I know," he said.

**I hope we can hold each other's hand when we get old one day. Even if there is only one cup of tea, we'll share it.**

The following afternoon I went to her house again. Standing before the door, hesitant, I heard the noise of a key again. The door opened, and she stood there with a bag of rubbish. She was shocked to see me. She said nothing, took the bag to the bin, and then re-entered the house. She tried to stop me coming in, but I forced my way in.

The house was just as it used to be, but the original study had been changed into a baby's room, with toys, a pram, small clothes, and a special baby smell. In our original room a bigger bed replaced the old one, a computer desk replaced her dresser, and on the desk were her reference books and jumbled materials. My friend had told me that she had little money. In her spare time she did some odd jobs for translation companies. Sometimes she had to leave the baby with a babysitter to do an interpreter's job away from home.

That day the baby was ill. My ex-wife ignored me to attend to the baby. Gazing at her profile, I had a complicated feeling. She was a good mother, definitely. She stared at the child with very soft lines in her face. I felt my eyes moistening. I recalled that she had once said to me: "Jin Yu, let's have a baby. I would like a girl. She would be very beautiful." But now she and the baby were both so pathetic.

After the baby took its medicine, she entrusted it to the babysitter, turned around and asked, "Why did you come here?"

"Just for a visit." I answered. She gave a very reluctant and scornful smile and said, "I have become a single mother, as you see. Her father abandoned her before she came into the world. You must be very happy now because I had bad luck after you left. Now you have seen everything you can go. We are busy."

I knew she hated me, but all of a sudden I felt very peaceful inside. She hadn't changed in any way; even her attitude to me hadn't changed when she spoke to me. She was just being stubborn.

I went into the kitchen. It hadn't changed much. The only difference was the child's stuff there. "I'll be back soon," I said, and then went to the market to buy fish, shrimps, vegetable and fruits—all things she had been fond of before. Then I went back. She didn't answer the door. The babysitter opened the door, and said, "She wants you to go away."

"Let me cook for you. I won't eat here. I will leave when the meal is ready." She could do nothing but let me in.

I went to the kitchen, and began to cook. At that moment I felt I was really at home. It even gave me the illusion of happiness. I imagined we were still a happy couple—she was playing with the baby in the living room and I was cooking for them. These thoughts brought tears. I had ruined the happiness that I could have owned. Now we had both changed. When I was cooking, she didn't come to me or say anything, which was different. Whenever I cooked before, she would stand at the kitchen door and talk to me. She used to be a talker, but now she was silent. I peeled the shrimps, minced them, put them into a small bowl, put the bowl on the table in the living room, and said: "Mix it with the child's food." She ignored me, and stared at the child playing on the sofa. The babysitter stood up, and said: "Let me serve the meal." She was wordless, but I saw her tears gushing.

"Come on. Let's eat together," the babysitter said. "No, thanks. I'll come tomorrow. Go ahead," I said. She made no reaction, and even when I left she didn't give me a glance. I gave a business card to the babysitter, and said, "If anything is wrong with the baby, call me. I will drive over here immediately."

I went directly to my lawyer friend's office and told him the whole process. He was sad at what I told him.

"Can you look after the baby?" he asked.

"Yes, I can," I said. "I don't mind. It doesn't matter even if she had many babies with many men. I'll take all of them if she allows me to."

"Why? Are you trying to make atonement?"

"No. Maybe I'm still in love with her. Now we are the same given that we each had a baby with someone else. No big deal. No. She didn't mind my son in those days."

"Then go for it. If you succeed, I'll arrange your wedding ceremony. That would be a wonderful story. You have made me believe in love again!"

Do you think I'm smart? I woke up her memory of the past, and reentered her life by cooking a meal. I want to tell you I didn't use any maneuver. I just wanted to cook nice food for her.

The next day, I went to cook for them again. The babysitter said, "She said you'd better not come again."

"I'll leave once the meal is ready. I won't eat here," I said. The result was the same as the previous day, the only difference being that her daughter called me "uncle" very happily.

On the fourth day, she came and stood at the kitchen door, finally. "Jin Yu, you shouldn't take so much trouble," she said.

"But I want to take care of you," I said. "I want you to have better food."

"You are mad. I have nothing to do with you now. I'm the ex-wife of another men and mother to his child. "

"You are wrong. You're my ex-wife, whomever you married. "

She got angry. "Get out of my house right now!" she cried.

"I know you hate me, and now I know I failed you, and I want to correct my mistakes," I explained.

She burst into tears, and said, "You mean you only found out that you were wrong after being dumped, and you have come back to apologize. I don't need your apology. If you weren't dumped, would you realize your mistakes?"

I was speechless, because she was right. If that woman hadn't left, how often would I have thought of my ex-wife? People change as the situation changes.

I stood there wordlessly. She turned off the gas and asked, "What the hell do you want to do?"

Suddenly my courage came back. "I want to remarry you," I said. "We can even date first. "

She walked out of the kitchen, and flung open the outside door. "Jin Yu, get out!" she commanded. "If you come here again I'll call the police. "

I went back several times in the next few days. I knocked on the door, but nobody answered.

One evening two months later the babysitter called me: "The baby has a bad fever. Can you come? We can't find a taxi. " I arrived there within 15 minutes. She suddenly felt relieved to see me. I spent the whole night with them at the Children's Hospital, and I stayed around the child when she was on a drip. She wanted me to go. "No," I said, "I'll wait here, and take you home. " She said nothing. Then I took them home, and said: "I'm leaving. Get some sleep. Tomorrow afternoon I will come to take you to the hospital again. " She didn't refuse.

Spring Festival was coming when the child recovered. I called my ex-wife, and asked what she wanted to eat during the Spring Festival. She said, "We are going to my parents' home to stay for a while. Don't come any more. "

After Spring Festival I was on a business trip for half a month. The first thing I did after coming back was to go to her place. But the babysitter gave me a letter saying she wouldn't allow me to enter the house any more.

I called her many times. Sometimes she didn't answer, and sometimes she told me she was busy. A few days ago, she finally chatted with me for a while. Perhaps she felt I was too boring. "Jin Yu," she said, "why do you keep coming back to me?"

"I know I don't deserve you," I said, "but if I hadn't gone off the rails I would never have known what kind of life and whom I really wanted. I ruined the happy life we could have had. Now I want to rebuild it."

She was silent for a while, and then said, "Now I have a baby. Have you thought about that?"

"Yes, I have," I said, "I'll treat her with love. Since her father doesn't love her, I'm willing to bring her up."

"Could you please tell me what kind of life you want?"

"I hope we can hold each other's hands when we get old one day. Even if there is only one cup of tea, we'll share it. Only you can give me such a life, and only I can give you that kind of life."

I meant it, and I wish I could make her believe me.

## Interviewer's Notes

### How Long Is It from the Destination Back to the Starting Point?

Before the interview with Jin Yu, I got some basic information about his story, which had already touched me. I have heard many marriage resumption stories, but he is the first man I've heard who chases his ex-wife who has remarried and divorced and become a single mother. I admire his courage. He needs not only to accept his ex-wife's remarriage but also the child of his ex-wife and another man. I told him frankly on the phone: "If you could get together again, you'd have a complicated identity." "Yes," he said. "Now I'm her ex-husband. After remarriage, I have to be her child's step-father. I'm willing to do it. We had been looking forward to a girl before."

I don't know how to depict his image. This forty-eight-year-old man has no facial wrinkles despite his harsh experiences, which is a miracle. He is a businessman with a rare elegance. I could imagine the encounter on that April morning many years ago. Maybe the young and innocent girl really couldn't resist his enthusiastic stare.

"Is it possible that when your ex-wife was your wife she depended on you with a touch of fear; for example, she was afraid of losing you and was worried your happy life couldn't continue for very long?" I asked him this out of politeness, but in fact I thought the answer would definitely be yes. Many an innocent woman devotes a lot to love a man and takes the man as the carrier of her life-long dream of happiness. The more they love, the more they fear; the more they fear, the more tightly they try to control the man. This kind of woman usually doesn't know that love can't stand too much strain, otherwise it might collapse.

My questions made him look sad. He said he knew what he meant to her. Like all lovers, when they decided to live together, their hearts were filled with hope and they had the same goal—a happy life. Two lovers are dreams to each other. When their dreams combine into one, they will make a very happy couple. However, he didn't cherish what he had. He broke his lover's dream, and his own dream was gone, too.

Jin Yu said life was like a puzzle, and one couldn't tell the starting point from the destination. Take his ex-wife for example. She and he were mutual starting points of their best love for each other, and now he hopes they can get together and turn the starting points into their destination.

I asked Jin Yu whether he was chasing her so intensely for atonement. He said yes and no. Yes, because he thought his ex-wife was in trouble due to his affair and if he had been faithful she wouldn't have suffered so much. No, because he believed firmly that confession and atonement were different; the former was the beginning of awareness, and the latter needed substantial acts, and without love the atonement path would be a very hard one. If he insists on atonement, he would like to make it on the premise of love.

I asked him to depict his ideal life. After a while he told me a story. A thief goes stealing on New Year's Eve. He sees several couples in different houses. In the first house a couple is quarrelling over the New Year's Eve dinner. In the second house is a couple sitting opposite each other. The man is drinking quietly, and the woman is dozing off. In the third house are two old people eating at the table. They eat and persuade each other to eat and drink. One of them says: "The fat for you. It's tasty. " The other says: "The lean for you. " The thief thinks to himself: "It must be a rich family. They are drinking and eating meat. This house will be my target. I'll get a good harvest today. " The thief doesn't enter the house until the old couple goes to sleep. Then he sees the food remaining on the table. It turns out that the so-called wine is just soup and the fat and lean are baked sweet potatoes respectively with red and white cores. The thief sighs to himself: "If I could live poor life so happily, I wouldn't need to be a thief. "

Jin Yu said that it took him 14 years to understand the simple truth of this story.

I used to be unsure whether this sad story belonged under such a magnificent title—*The Chinese Dream*. So I eliminated it, and picked it back over and over. It would break my heart if I couldn't put it here. It is a mature season when a man is 48 years old. At 48, Barack Obama became president. But maybe Jin Yu, 48 years old, too, doesn't have the same magnificent ideal. His dream is just to get back his lover and family. Everybody has his or her own life dream, and everyone is equal as long as he or she works hard to realize his or her dream and to harvest happiness. From the viewpoint of ordinary people, Obama's dream is a miracle, and Jin Yu's experience is a lesson that might be useful to us; after witnessing Obama's miracle, we still have to hold the hands of our lovers and children and go back to our ordinary life. There is a Chinese saying: "Self-cultivation, regulating the family, governing the country and establishing peace throughout the world. " For a small potato it is a life-long career to regulate his or her family, and sometimes he or she may not do it well for life. If someone incidentally has the same thing in mind as Jin Yu, then maybe this story can be of special meaning to him or her. Life is not long, so it is better to understand something early than late. This is true of many people, including Jin Yu.

# *Half Soft and Half Strong*

**Time of interview**: July 6, 2008

**Place**: Starbucks Coffee, Beijing World Trade Center

Shi Fumao, male, was born in Wei County, Hebei Province in March 1974. Shi worked in a flour-processing factory in Xingtai after graduating from the law department of Hebei University in 1996. He passed the bar examination in 1997, and became a full-time lawyer with the Jiaxin Law Firm in 1998. Shi co-founded Hebei Junhexin Law Firm with another partner in 2002. He then became the senior partner and deputy director of the firm, and was awarded the title of "excellent lawyer" by the local justice administration. From July 1, 2004 till now, Shi Fumao has been working as a public interest lawyer with the Beijing Zhicheng Law Firm and Beijing Juvenile Legal Aid and Research Center. He has also been the general secretary of the Committee for Legal Aid and Public Interest of the All-China Lawyers Association and the executive director of the Beijing Migrant Workers Legal Aid Work Station.

**I certainly had an opportunity to bring home more money when working as a private lawyer. However, I always felt very sad about those financially stressed people struggling at the bottom of society, as they failed to ensure their legitimate rights and interests just because they couldn't afford to hire lawyers.**

I am a public interest lawyer. You've seen my business card with "legal aid" on it. Aid means that we get no pay. I used to be a full-time lawyer providing legal aid to juveniles and minors, and now I mainly focus on offering legal assistance to migrant workers; of course, for free. My salary is around 2,500 yuan, and I can make about 4,000 yuan with overtime pay and subsidies. As the executive director of the work station, I and the director, also a partner, get the highest salary. He's very famous; you may have heard of him. He could earn tens of millions a year if he worked as a private lawyer. His name is Tong Lihua. Frankly, I may not have come to Beijing to work as a public interest lawyer without Tong.

Have you seen lots of lawyers making big money? Yes, talented people in this industry can definitely become rich. Private lawyers are much needed in more business fields, and they get more chances to earn big money thanks to the country's rapid socio-economic development. You asked me whether I had ever thought of being a private lawyer? Well, I used to be such a lawyer. I was a partner in a law firm in Xingtai, Hebei Province, my hometown. I brought home 60,000 or 70,000 yuan a year at that time. It was a pretty good income in such a small city in the year of 2000. My wife worked at the Industrial and Commercial Bank of China, and she also had a good salary. We were pretty well off in the local area, and bought ourselves an apartment. Actually, housing prices in my hometown were really low. An apartment in Beijing costs at least a million yuan. I bought a 100-square-meter apartment for less than 100,000 yuan in my hometown. When I worked as a public interest lawyer later, I was far from well paid compared to the amount of work I had to do. I accepted dozens of cases every year, and one third of them was handled gratis. I gathered the evidence and covered the court cases myself. My teacher, also one of my partners, joked, "You should at least demand a token payment—800 yuan each at the minimum." All the partners I have had so far have been supportive of my work.

When working as a private lawyer I always felt very sad about those financially stressed people struggling at the bottom of society, as they failed to protect their legitimate rights and interests due to the high attorney fees. As a result, I didn't have the heart to charge such people, regardless of the nature of the case, whether it was simple or complex. At the same time, I was also wondering whether I should set up a special public organ to safeguard the rights of the vulnerable groups, and became part of it, as the society needs public interest lawyers. What I had thought about for years became a reality after a heart-to-heart conversation with Tong Lihua in Beijing in 2004.

So I feel most comfortable with the current situation; it suits my personality and conscience. The legal aid station I work for has clearly stated that no lawyer is allowed to collect fees. You know, the service we provide here is completely free of charge. Instead of collecting commission fees from the clients, our salary and funding sources are mainly subsidies from the government, financial aid from legal aid foundations, and donations from public organs and individuals, including grants from the United Nations. As a lawyer, I am well provided with food and clothing. My modest income is enough to maintain a basic lifestyle. I don't need to calculate how much commission I can get from each case, or how I should charge different cases. All I have to do is a good job on the case itself. I don't even have to tell my clients how much they should pay me. Instead, I always say, "Don't be afraid. Please tell me what you require, and I will do whatever it takes to help you. The service is free." You know how good I feel about this? It makes me feel that what I am doing is pure and lofty, with no self-interest involved.

I was once asked whether I wanted to make a fortune. I replied, "Would you believe me if I said no?" Some people, probably the vast majority, may not believe me. Anyway, I always say what is in my mind. And I feel that making a fortune may not help people feel happier in the current social situation. Money sometimes can be a troublemaker. When a man or a family has a large amount of money beyond their basic needs, problems may keep cropping up, such as family disharmony, extravagant life, children's delinquency, poor relations, and no support for the elderly. Problems may crop up in bunches. Haven't we seen or heard too much of these things? Frankly, I don't want my life to be ruined and controlled by money. Of course, the life I have chosen will definitely not bring me a fortune, yet I'm satisfied with a simple life, a harmonious family and a diligent and hard-working child. Time is far from enough for a person devoted to the career he loves. How can he have any spare time? Is it necessary to get a great deal of money if one has no time to spend it? Some people would definitely laugh at me after hearing me say this. My ideas actually conform to those of many people, and I am not holding myself aloof. Frankly speaking, I'm quite well known in the industry after being a lawyer for many years. I have received many honors, published books, and handled cases successfully in recent years. My career prospects wouldn't be gloomy if I went back to being a private lawyer. But I've never been tempted to do so. I like my life the way it is right now, as I work voluntarily. I also feel satisfied with a stable life, my ever-growing competence and a growing range of clients. What more could I ask for?

**A good lawyer, in my view, should be kind and selfless, put aside personal interests to help the poor get fair treatment, and plead for justice on behalf of the people. That was the career prospect I set for myself when I chose to study law.**

One's life ideal is definitely not shaped for no reason. My ideas and the special feeling towards migrant workers are probably related to my family, education and work experience.

I was born into a peasant's family. My father used to be a teacher at a privately-run school. His stubbornness finally got him fired, as he offended the leadership. Then he worked on a construction site for more than three decades. He was at first a common worker, and then became a surveyor, because he could read and write, and understand technical drawings. But he was still a migrant worker in fact. My brother worked for a construction company as a migrant worker. I was the only person to attend college in my family. Though my father was no longer a teacher, he insisted on sending me to college. All my summer and winter holidays were spent on construction sites from the high school entrance examination till the year I graduated from college. I had to earn money to pay my tuition so that my father could save money for the family. I was familiar with various jobs, and I knew exactly which job was dangerous, or which was the most difficult one. I ate and drank with migrant workers, and worked with them in sun and wind. I knew how hard they worked and how fatigued they were, and I heard a lot of their heart-rending stories. They worked away from home, leaving their wives and children. I felt that they were just like my family, really. I have often thought that I too would have become a migrant worker if my father hadn't insisted on me going to college. It's possible that I might have had to wait for my pay and might have had to forgo trips home during the holidays in order to save money.... You know for this reason, I always go out of my way to offer legal aid to migrant workers. I've never looked down upon them, as I'm keenly aware of what they suffer. It makes my heart ache to hear their miserable stories. A good lawyer, in my view, should possess many good qualities, among which being kind and selfless should be the most important. They should also put aside their personal interests to help the poor get fair treatment. That is what people called " pleading for justice on behalf of the people. " That was also the career I set for myself when I chose to study law.

I was a laborer before I became a lawyer. After graduating from university, I was assigned to work in a flour factory. As I had a degree in law, they assigned me to the security section. When I wrote advice on the labor laws on a bulletin blackboard, the leadership was alarmed. They used to get all the staff to work overtime for free, but I was telling them to ask for the overtime pay. I was still too young to understand the complexity of society. I felt particularly bored in the security division, and applied to join the party at that time. The leader said, "How about going into the workshop? " I thought it would be better if I went there. I should try to learn more as I was already in the factory. I was then transferred to the flour-making workshop. I earned more, and worked three shifts. My income quickly doubled, and I earned over 1,200 yuan every month, a pretty handsome salary in Xingtai. It was roughly at that time that I met my wife.

I also passed the bar examination during this period. Making flour was not what I wanted to do with my life. Though I was earning a good salary, I still wanted to be a lawyer, or I wouldn't have chosen to learn law. I watched lots of movies and soap operas when I was young. I was greatly impressed by the way lawyers in the movies and soap operas always sought justice for the victims. I felt that this job was a lofty calling. So I resigned from the factory, and went to work for a law firm. Someone said that I was foolish to give up such a good job and a lucrative salary. Many people were eager to work at the flour factory, but couldn't get hired. After I left the factory, I began to know that every person knows best what he or she wants. I fully realized what that meant when I quit my job as a private lawyer in Xingtai and chose to be a public interest lawyer in Beijing. Life is actually composed of choices. One man's meat is another man's poison. You should follow the voice inside you, as it is your own life. Your choices make you live the way you want to live. So no one can be replaced, or eventually be controlled by others.

The first case I handled turned into a legal aid one, and I received only 800 yuan. I would not even have received that money if the legal firm hadn't made it a minimum requirement. I know very well that it's very difficult for ordinary people to pursue a lawsuit. As a former migrant worker myself, I know exactly how hard it is for a migrant worker to earn money, and what he has to suffer. I accepted the case on April 22, 1999, and it took a whole four years to complete. The case was a joint-venture dispute, with a private factory on one side and a state-owned food company on the other. The two sides reached a consensus on cooperation. According to the agreement, the factory provided the building and equipment, while the food company provided the capital and staff. Then the food company ended the cooperation unilaterally, fearing gloomy prospects and sluggish business. As a result, the private company suffered a great loss. This case had already dragged on for several years before I took over. It was returned for retrial many times. The owner of the private factory came to me, and said that he had no money. I felt what he said was true as he looked so exhausted. I couldn't bear to ask for a fee when he was so desperate. I said, "It doesn't matter. I will take the case, and you can pay me after we win the lawsuit." Then I said to the law firm: "Just charge him the minimum fee—800 yuan. My client will pay the rest after we win the lawsuit." I spared no effort in this thankless case, and it was returned for retrial again and again. Yet I got a windfall from this incident. I wrote an article titled, "The Number of Retrials Should be Restricted," which caused a sensation after it was published, and even attracted the attention of the Supreme People's Court, *Legal Daily* and judicial circles as a whole. The two courts in charge of this case were also criticized in a circular sent by the Hebei Provincial Higher People's Court, and the Supreme People's Court made a judicial interpretation of the "Regulations on Returned Retrial and Ordered Retrial of Civil Cases of People's Courts" on July 31, 2002, stating that the same civil case shall only be returned for retrial once. This was the first time I felt that a lawyer's job was not just to safeguard the legitimate rights and interests of the clients; he also had an obligation and responsibility to put forward suggestions for legislation which would benefit people.

I was wary of writing articles before, but this incident convinced me that a lawyer, besides profound expertise and rich practical experience, should also be equipped with excellent writing skills and strong summing-up capability. These skills can be achieved only after unremitting thinking and aggressive exploration in one's work. I began to practice my writing skills, and tried to get articles I wrote published. I thought that this was one way to support the development of our country's legal system.

After this case, I realized that I was destined not to make big money as a lawyer. I didn't know why the cases I handled always became legal aid ones. I might have been fated to meet these people. Another case involved a 16-year-old girl who went to work at a paper mill without a labor contract. She suffered an accident only 12 days later, when she lost half of one arm. This was identified as a level-four disability. Her employer only agreed to pay the costs of her hospitalization, not the other expenses, due to the lack of a labor contract. The girl was later introduced to me. I agreed to handle the case. Then I gradually learned that the employer was fairly powerful, in other words, it would be difficult for us to win the case, even though it was not complicated. In fact, that company had some special social relations. Xingtai is actually a small place, with complicated and deep-rooted social ties. Lawyers are always reluctant to accept such cases, as they earn little and may offend powerful people. But I felt duty-bound to help her. I don't like to talk big, nor am I a noble person; yet I have one merit, and that is stubbornness, or persistence. I believe in fairness and justice, and I think lawyers are born to safeguard and achieve fairness and justice, so I am not afraid to offend someone. It took rather a long time to handle this case, and I only charged her 800 yuan. She eventually got over 160,000 yuan in compensation. Though the money could not buy her another arm, it could at least make her life a bit easier.

I added a new area to my business after this case—juvenile legal aid, or protecting the legitimate rights and interests of minors. Besides providing legal aid to migrant workers, I am now committed to the protection of minors.

**It was a turning point in my life when I became a public interest lawyer in Beijing. I don't have to consider whether my job can generate income for my colleagues any more; all I have to do is to provide service to my clients with my own expertise, which brings me great pleasure!**

What really propelled me to provide legal aid to migrant workers was the case related to payments in arrears for 173 migrant workers. This case also happened in Xingtai in 2001. A contractor from Guangzong County, Hebei Province, came to me at that time. He had formed a plastering team with 172 farmers from his hometown. They worked in the city, and got no pay at the end of the project. The migrant workers, however, could not figure out who should pay them, the construction company or the contractor. Every day they argued with the man who had taken them away from their hometown. The contractor was so miserable as he was threatened every day, and he really had no money. He went to the construction company and the project owner every day, with no result. His father was around 60, and worked at the Guangzong Trade and Industry Bureau. The contractor's fellow-villagers went to the old man every day, urging him to get his son to pay them, or they would wreck his house. The old man called me frequently after I took the case. The construction contractor and the project owner finally paid the workers in full. The contractor's father went specifically to Xingtai to see me, and said, "Mr. Shi, you have saved my whole family." The case was neither complicated nor difficult, yet it sticks in my mind even now. It was the old man who made me feel a sense of job satisfaction. When your limited effort can actually help so many people, you know, that feeling is really awesome.

I handled many similar cases in Xingtai, and I gradually became a bit famous. I was already a well-known legal aid lawyer in Xingtai. We set up a legal aid hotline there, which was still available when I left Xingtai for Beijing. The hotline is still there, even now. I also got opportunities to engage in various activities for experience sharing, attended meetings in Beijing, and met some lawyers doing the same kind of work. I came to know Tong Lihua through the meetings. As a renowned public interest lawyer in Beijing, Tong is committed to offering legal aid to adults and migrant workers. The image of public interest lawyers set by Tong has exerted a sound impact on the whole of society. We often exchanged ideas, and shared the same ambitions and purposes. He invited me to leave Xingtai for Beijing to join him in 2004, and I agreed without any hesitation. I think it was a critical turning point in my life as I don't have to consider whether what I do can generate income for my colleagues—all I have to do is to provide service to my clients with my own expertise, which brings me great pleasure!

It was easier said than done to leave a place you have lived in for 30 years. I thought I'd found the thing I should do and a way to realize my ideal. Yet I had my own family, my wife and my son. I couldn't just go anywhere any time I wanted to. It was not just a brief stay in one place; instead, I had to move the whole family to Beijing. It meant that we had to make a living in this strange city. Besides, after joining the team of public interest lawyers, I would really have no opportunity to create a prosperous life for my family.

I would like to thank my wife, as she has accompanied me in my poor life, yet she has never complained. To help me realize my ideal, she gave up quite a good job in our hometown, and sold our apartment. She lives together with me in a 30-square-meter rented house, and has raised and educated our child all by herself. I knew that she left Xingtai with mixed feelings, yet she did not complain, just shedding tears in silence.

I became a public interest lawyer on July 1, 2004 and started completely from scratch. I was an experienced lawyer in Xingtai, but I even had to learn the way Beijingers talk when I first came to Beijing. I had to become familiar with this city, the roads here, and the way people live and work. I had to adjust to new conditions gradually. I could serve people here better only after I knew more about the city.

Sometimes I think I have a strong capability for work. I began to handle cases independently on July 21, 20 days after arriving in Beijing.

I don't know whether you have had contact with real migrant workers, who live at the bottom of society. They build high-rise buildings, but no single corner belongs to them. Their job is really tough and dirty, even dangerous. Sometimes they are vulnerable to work-related injuries, or even lose their lives due to insufficient safety measures. They also often have a problem of unpaid wages. They can't go home due to lack of money after working hard all the year round. These people are our clients. We help protect and fight for their legitimate rights and interests, and teach them how to deal with problems rationally when they are treated unfairly, and how to use legal weapons to protect themselves. They have to be restrained from running wild or doing something to endanger public security and disrupting social order, and even committing crimes. We have stopped many migrant workers protesting to the higher authorities or staging sit-down strikes, and have shown them how to fight for their legitimate rights and interests in a proper way.

Here's one example. In 2004, a migrant worker from Hebei Province was introduced to me. He and his colleagues had not been paid for their work. What he had experienced was typical. He had been beaten and threatened many times, and complained to the higher authorities, all to no avail. The man was finally so depressed that he drank chicken blood with his companions, and they vowed to kill the boss and then deliver themselves up to justice. At the very beginning, he didn't believe that we could help him nor we would do it for free. He gradually came to trust us after he saw us gathering evidence, regardless of threats and any personal gain or loss. We finally won the case, and later agreed that without the help of public interest lawyers many migrant workers might resort to violence to redress their grievances. This man later helped promote relevant legal knowledge among his fellow migrant workers. As a result, violent disputes caused by failure to pay wages have been avoided.

In fact, many cases concerning migrant workers are related to the Labor Contract Law. We completed a sensational case some time ago. It was a labor dispute between an ordinary migrant worker and Kentucky Fried Chicken (KFC). Xu Yange, from Shandong Province, had worked for KFC since 1995. KFC required all storage employees to be dispatched by a labor services company in 2003. Xu was fired by KFC in 2005, and the company refused to pay compensation to Xu, claiming that Xu was not a permanent employee of the company. We legal aid lawyers collected a great deal of material concerning KFC's employment system, and finally reached an agreement with KFC China after intensive and tough investigations and evidence collection, application for arbitration and a lawsuit. What we did provided a satisfactory solution for Xu Yange and other clients. Besides, KFC also promised that the labor dispatch system would be halted except in special circumstances, and the former dispatched employees would be made regular staff, and their former length of service would still be counted. This case will benefit thousands of KFC Chinese workers financially.

We often encounter some danger, perhaps due to the special nature of the clients we serve. Sometimes we are threatened or otherwise intimidated. Sometimes we can not collect evidence alone, due to the lack of guaranteed safety. My colleagues and I were once surrounded by dozens of hooligans wearing T-shirts of the same color and shoes of the same style. We were undeterred even at that time because much more vulnerable migrant workers needed protection and assistance. I even received a call from a migrant worker around 9 p. m. one night before the Spring Festival. I was told that some 50 workers had clashed with their boss on the construction site. Though it was not a lawyer's responsibility to break up a fight, yet our sense of professional ethics drove another lawyer and me to rush to the site at midnight. The boss finally agreed to pay 55 workers 47,000 yuan, and we left around 3 a. m. the next day.

**What we do actually protects the legitimate rights and interests of tens of thousands of migrant workers, and brings warmth and confidence to their families. A great number of contradictions have been resolved, and the seeds of harmony have been planted. We have done our part to help build a harmonious society, which makes me feel very useful and meaningful.**

I am often moved by the people I serve. They are simple at heart, though neither rich nor well educated. But they know precisely what to love and what to hate. They know how to repay your kindness. We do not charge them any fee, yet every time we win a case and get wages or compensation for work-related injuries for our clients, they always give us money as a token of appreciation. Of course we do not take this money, even though they try to press it on us. And we have much trouble sending the money back. I think this is not simply a matter of money, but a sincere feeling among people.

These incidents are an incentive to keep me moving on. Every time I go to the office at 7 a. m. , there are always cases waiting for me, which I do not have the heart to neglect. Others may not be able to understand what I feel, yet people who have once worked here would know exactly what I have experienced. Many lawyers who have worked here have experienced the poor and busy life of public interest lawyers, yet no one left due to financial reasons. It may be some kind of cohesion. Tong Lihua and I have discussed this issue, and we held that it was normal if someone left. Just as I put it, everyone knows exactly what he wants. On top of that, we are gratified that the lawyers who have worked here possessed a strong and tested moral quality.

The Legal Aid Work Station for Migrant Workers is a specialized agency, with professional and full-time lawyers working here. Besides supervision by the government, we lawyers keep very strict discipline, such as the "eight musts" and "eight prohibitions. " According to the regulations, we are required to identify cases clearly, make a record of the cases, and sum up the cases after finishing them. Full-time lawyers are subject to double supervision as a way to effectively guarantee the quality of legal aid cases.

Obviously, the power of one man is pretty limited. We must get more people to join the team of public interest lawyers to meet the legal needs of migrant workers all over the country. As the general secretary of the Committee of Legal Aid and Public Interest of the All-China Lawyers Association, I have always been active in promoting the legal aid model of the Beijing Legal Aid Work Station. Supported by the Ministry of Justice and the Ministry of Commerce and financed by the China Legal Aid Foundation and the United Nations Development Programme as well as the concerted efforts of the National Lawyers Association and various provincial lawyers associations, legal aid work stations for migrant workers are now operating in over 20 provinces, and a team composed of professional and full-time lawyers is taking shape. The team is being created to provide legal assistance for migrant workers. Lawyers in China are now playing an increasingly important role in providing legal aid to migrant workers.

If a migrant worker gets hurt on the job, and his boss is reluctant to shoulder the responsibility, the former may ask his friends to attack the boss. Similarly, some worker may threaten to cut off one of the boss's hands if his own hand has been injured at work. Many similar cases have been nipped in the bud through the considerable efforts of our lawyers. Our legal aid work station has handled a total of 155 cases of unpaid wages concerning migrant workers, with a total of 3,620 migrant workers involved. Of the migrant workers who have received our help, not one went to the government for help, and all cases have been handled properly. What we have done actually has protected the legitimate rights and interests of tens of thousands of migrant workers, and brought warmth and confidence to their families. A great number of contradictions have been resolved, and the seeds of harmony have been planted. We have played our part to help build a harmonious society, which makes me feel very valuable and meaningful.

I feel very satisfied with what I am doing now, and my only regret is that, due to my increased workload, I have little time to write down what I have felt and experienced over many years. I can only do this after my retirement. My biggest wish now is to get more people to join us, and create a task force of professional lawyers to safeguard the rights and interests of migrant workers through concerted efforts. Those ordinary workers, who have made great contributions to the development of society, should be well protected and prevented from being bullied. We should also make great endeavors to promote relevant legislation, so that migrant workers can be treated equally and be protected by law. I hope that what we are doing can help benefit more workers. My colleagues and I have always been working on this.

## Interviewer's Notes

### Walking with the Sword of Justice

A headline titled "Soliciting Opinions on Legal Aid Regulation Draft from the General Public Again—Migrant Workers Struggling for Unpaid Wages Can Apply for Free Legal Aid" was carried on the front page of the *Beijing Youth Daily* on July 8, 2008. I don't know how Shi Fumao felt after seeing this news. He has been committed to providing free legal assistance to migrant workers for five years.

A group of figures can show the work intensity of Shi Fumao and his colleagues. From 2005 till now, lawyers working at the Beijing Legal Aid Work Station for Migrant Workers have received 15,645 cases via personal calls, visits and online consulting, with 81,017 migrant workers and over 450 million yuan involved. The work station has provided assistance to 4,124 people, with 39.05 million yuan involved. All this work was completed in less than three years.

Shi Fumao is a workaholic, starting work at 7 a.m. every morning, and never knowing when the day's work will end. On the day I interviewed him, for instance, he offered legal training to migrant workers that evening in Shijiazhuang. He was at his office in Beijing before 8 a.m. the next day to collect materials for a case regarding unpaid wages.

Shi Fumao took a taxi on the day appointed for the interview, fearing a possible traffic jam. It was unusual for him, as he prefers to go everywhere by bus or subway. He goes to work by bicycle, as he cannot afford a car. Many of his old classmates and friends now own luxury cars and good apartments. Many of them even earn millions as lawyers. If he had not chosen to be a public lawyer, he would be one of them. But now he only owns a bicycle. His apartment doesn't belong to him yet, as he has to pay back a housing loan every month.

So our interview started with money. Money and welfare, two contradictory yet inseparable concepts. You can not earn big money while bringing welfare to the public. Yet what kind of public welfare can you provide without money? The legal aid work station Shi works at has clearly stated that migrant workers are not allowed to pay for meals when consulting with lawyers. Where did this money come from? Public interest lawyers also have to support their families and have meals every day. With great emotion, Shi Fumao expressed his admiration and appreciation for his partner Tong Lihua, who sold his own apartment to support the public welfare service he is devoted to. "I can't hold a candle to Mr. Tong. He represents the best social image of lawyers—honest, just, nice and dedicated," said Shi. Actually, Shi is also evaluated in this way by people he has helped. According to Shi Fumao, Tong Lihua is his mentor and intimate friend. Tong evaluated Shi as follows: "Shi Fumao is an outstanding lawyer who has been active in devoting himself to his social responsibilities at the expense of his personal interests for years. He has been working from dawn to dusk, devoting himself to his career and the work station. Instead of being deterred by threats and intimidation, he has always fought for the interests of migrant workers. He has now emerged as a renowned expert in cases relating to migrant workers after intensive study and research in this regard. He has handled a large number of cases. Shi contributed to leading the lawyers of the Beijing Legal Aid Work Station for Migrant Workers to safeguard the legitimate rights and interests of tens of thousands of migrant workers and bring warm and confidence to their families, and resolved a large number of contradictions while planting the seeds of harmony. Those lawyers played their part in helping to create a more harmonious and beautiful Beijing. Shi has already established a good image of a socialist legal worker with his down-to-earth efforts."

This is an era of material temptations. Many people and their stories tell us that people can not control the ever-expanding desire for materials due to the vulnerability rooted in human nature. As a result, sordid stories related to desire keep cropping up. I was refreshed and gratified after my conversation with Shi Fumao. His feelings, his pursuit of a simple and virtuous life, his great care for others and his professional accomplishments came over clearly. Such people are living all around us, serving the public silently, regardless of personal gain or loss. As the saying goes, "Peaches and plums do not have to talk, yet the world beats a path to them."

Shi Fumao says that his largest collection so far is of judgments and mediation decisions. He keeps the legal documents related to each case. For cases with hundreds of clients, he has to collect a great pile of documents, with one file for each client. Large files can be seen everywhere in his home and office. They are not only a record of his work, but also a record of what happened between the clients and him. More importantly, the people he encountered briefly have finally come to live a contented life and found a way back home thanks to what he has done.

The last topic of that day may seem like the start of the interview, yet I don't know why I put it forward at the end of our dialogue. I asked him why he chose to study law and become a lawyer. He attributed it to many novels he read and movies he saw when he was young, and felt that a lawyer was like a heroic knight walking with a sword, brave in taking responsibility on his shoulders. I asked whether he had realized that dream of being a knight now, and he replied that only when all migrant workers are happy will his own dream be realized. Shi Fumao rushed to catch the subway after these words, as he was on duty to receive hotline calls in the afternoon, with a great deal of thorny cases to be handled. I thought about his metaphor of walking with a sword while looking at him as he departed. I felt that in the heart of this modern lawyer, who gave up the opportunity to earn big money, there must be a "sword" forged by love and justice.

# Relay of Mother and Daughter, Dreaming of Being a Star

**Time of interview**: November 28, 2008

**Place**: Shanghai Saloon, Yi Zhuang, Beijing

Zhou Yiwei, female, 44 years old, graduated with a major in preschool education. She has worked as a teacher in a kindergarten, and as a music teacher in a primary school. Now she is working as an office director in a private cultural dissemination company.

**In my mind I have always had the same dream as my daughter, that is, to become an actress.**

Yesterday, I celebrated my 44th birthday. I spent it with my husband and daughter. My husband said that after 40 every birthday is very special for a woman. So we decided to spend the day at home. We bought some shrimps, and I made noodles with gravy. My husband and daughter bought a birthday cake for me. The total income of myself and my husband is less than 8,000 yuan, and we spend 3,500 yuan a month for the mortage on our apartment. Except for daily expenses, the rest of the income is basically spent on my daughter. My daughter takes classes in ancient zither, piano and foreign languages. In addition, there are all kinds of fees that have to be paid to the school. Money seems to flow away like water.

The school that my daughter goes to is a special school for learning film and TV performing. She wants to be an actress. It is her ideal, and it was also my ideal when I was young. My daughter is very pretty. When a mother praises her own child like this, other people may think that it is because of her partiality. The more you observe your child, the more you feel that he or she is pleasing to the eye. But, in fact, all the people who have seen my daughter say that she is pretty, much prettier than I was when I was young. My daughter acted in a TV play when she was only five years old, and she has learned dancing since she was six. She has a good figure. She has had parts in many films and TV plays. Everyone who has seen her in films or TV plays thinks that she looks good on screen.

Another reason for saving money is that I want my daughter to take the entrance examination for the Beijing Film Academy in 2010. I met a man whose daughter failed the entrance examination for the Beijing Film Academy. Previously, he had spent more than 30,000 yuan on cultural classes, at a teacher's urging. However, it was judged that the girl's chest was "too high." This is a saying in the acting profession. There is a special kind of girl who grows like this. Though she is not fat at all, it seems that the upper part of the body is too fat. You know, when people are on the screen, they tend to be broadened. People of ordinary build will appear fatter on the screen. Those who look slim and comely on the screen look skinny in real life. The teacher recommended a slimming clinic, and the girl's father spent another 60,000 yuan.

My parents were engaged in scientific work, and had no connection with the arts. My only brother went to the US after graduating from college, and he is still there. When I was a little girl, my brother and I lived with my grandma and grandpa in Beijing while my parents were working in Lanzhou. My grandma was an interesting old lady. She was a Shanghainese. My grandpa was a professor in a university. My grandma never worked, and it was said that she was from a capitalist family. She was fond of good food and clothes. I remember her cutting clothing patterns while singing along with Shaoxing Opera tunes. She was good at making clothes, and she dressed me up like a doll.

Perhaps it was grandma's influence that has made me treat my own daughter like a big doll. My mother disapproved, saying that I was spoiling the girl. She warned me that such girls tended not to be content, but had unrealistic expectations from life. She concluded that I failed in the college entrance examination and was a daydreamer because I had been spoiled by my grandma.

Dad also spoiled me very much, just as my husband spoils my daughter, and says that so long as she is happy and grows up to be a contented housewife that is all that matters. Grandma used to say that my good looks would bring me good fortune, but she was wrong. I haven't got any professional skill. I work in public relations, relying on my gift of the gab to earn a living. As a pretty girl, I didn't study well. And then, later, when I dreamed of being an actress, I neglected my studies even more.

**One day two men who were going to shoot a film came to our school. One of them was a teacher at the Beijing Film Academy. They wanted to recruit a girl who was good at English, and one of the teachers recommended me.**

As the prettiest girl in my school, I was always chosen to present flowers to guests. I was also good at singing and recitation, so I was always the leading singer in the school choir. I learned recitation at the local Children's Palace. It was due to being close to my recitation teacher that I first encountered the concept of divorce, as the teacher was a single mother.

When I was in middle school, I was good at English. My teacher knew this. When I was awarded prizes in the English competitions, she used to give me a little bottle of perfume. She reminded me of my grandma. Unfortunately, I gradually lost touch with her.

When the teacher at the Children's Palace recommended me to the two film makers, I was in awe, but nowadays children are very mercenary. If they are asked to star in an advertising film, they ask such questions as "How much will you pay? Does it include tax? How many seconds do I have to appear on the screen?" They are all very professional, whereas when I was in middle school I felt it was a great honor to get such a chance.

Grandma said they had come when I was away and left a phone number for me to call them. She urged me to give it a try because not everyone could have this chance. It was a special day. I had a shower and put on a beautiful dress.

Except for sportswear, all my clothes were made by my grandma. Then Grandma asked me to sit in front of a mirror and dressed me up carefully. Then she looked at me as though appreciating a piece of artwork. That evening, she stayed with me when I called the teacher of the Beijing Film Academy, and congratulated me when he said he would come and pick me up in a car.

It was a sleepless night for both me and Grandma. She was very talkative, telling me many things about her childhood, such as how she followed her mum to go to the cinema and eat Western-style food, how her mum bought cloth and got a tailor to make clothes out of it, how she attended dancing party and how she had blind dates. Suddenly I discovered that Grandma was not a woman whose ideal would be a housewife. In fact, she had her own dreams, but she had had no chance to realize them.

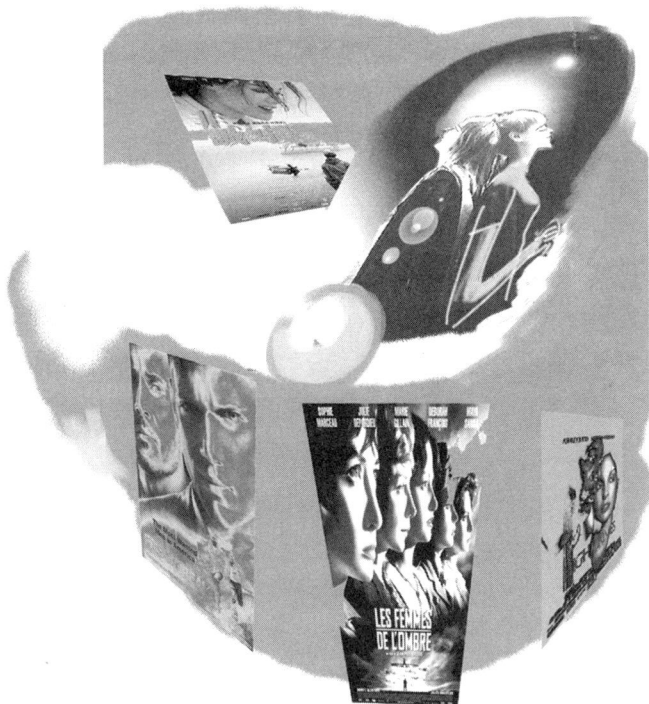

I got up quite late the next morning. When I got up I found that Grandma had prepared a skirt for me. She had made it out of fine cotton cloth with a pattern of white and yellow peonies. The neckline and lower border were decorated with lace.

I met the teacher from the Beijing Film Academy, and also two foreigners, who were the producer and vice-director. They asked me questions in English, such as "What about your family? Have you ever seen a Hollywood movie? Where did you buy your skirt?" In answer to the last question, I told them that my grandma had made it specially.

But three months later, the Beijing Film Academy teacher called to say that the movie makers had found a more suitable candidate, as I was too old to play the role of a 12- or 13-year-old girl. Nevertheless, she encouraged me to take the entrance examination for the Academy.

**When I was a girl, my dream remained in my mind; I was too timid to realize it. Maybe it is different today.**

Now I am over 40 years old, but I still take a passionate interest in movies. Sometimes when I watch a movie, I imagine how I could act a role in it.

When I told my mother that I intended to take the entrance examination for the Academy, she replied, "When did anyone in our family dream of being an actress? Why not take the examination for a circus?" My mum always treated me and my brother in an exaggerated way; when she was satisfied with us, she would lavish praise on us, but when she was not satisfied with us, she would scold us roundly.

I was very angry at the time, but when my father advised me to study for a profession that would give me a lifetime career, I finally had to agree. To hold a job that lasts only as long as one's youth is not a secure way to earn a living.

Because of parental pressure, I missed enrolling at the Beijing Film Academy and the Central Academy of Drama. I missed my chance forever.

My daughter says that her ideal is to attend the Beijing Film Academy, no matter how many times she has to take the entrance examinations. She has her own ideas and her definite views. She will sacrifice a lot for her ideal, and may do many silly things.

After I graduated from a teachers-training school, I was assigned to a kindergarten. There was a little girl there who was very pretty, and I treated her very well. At first, I didn't pay much attention to her, but when I learned that her grandfather was a TV actor I began to pay attention to her and treated her very well almost instinctively. Maybe it was because I too wanted to appear on TV.

There was another silly thing that I did. One day, I heard that a Hong Kong film star whom I very much admired was to come to Beijing. Now, the father of one of the children at the kindergarten worked at Beijing Capital Airport. When he came to pick up his child, I asked him to take me to meet that famous man. He agreed. On that day, I asked for leave from the kindergarten, and went to the airport. He took me right out onto the parking apron, and when the film star disembarked, I ran towards him and told him that I was a fan of his. I even got a photo taken with him. I have kept that photo ever since. I have never shown it to my daughter or my husband, but after they read your article, they will know about it. Everyone who once had a dream can understand it.

**In the second year of my marriage my daughter was born. Then I thought that the ambition that I hadn't realized in my own life could be realized by my daughter for me.**

I mentioned before that the dream of being an actress influenced me greatly. Now let me tell you that I married my husband just because he reminded me of that Hong Kong film idol whom I met at the airport. My husband is the director of a small department in a housing administration, but he does look like the film star.

My husband treats me very well, and he treats my daughter especially well. In that sense, my marriage is happy, though we are not rich, and we have to work hard to earn a living.

My husband was quite open-minded about the baby, saying that he would love it no matter whether it was a boy or a girl, as long as he or she was healthy. I had a Caesarean birth. When the child was born, the doctor said to me, "Congratulations! You have a baby girl." An idea flashed into my mind: Thank God for treating me so well; all my life's ambition can be realized by my daughter for me!

Many people have tried to persuade me not to let my daughter take the entrance examination for the Beijing Film Academy. Someone even said, "You are pushing your daughter into an abyss of suffering. It is rumored that some actresses sell themselves to become famous. And then there's the nude photo scandal, mobile phone scandal, etc." I also worry about this, but I think I am still driven by my unrealized dream.

I am over 40, and I am beginning to understand why my mother wanted me to acquire a professional skill, and not rely only on my good looks. I am also beginning to understand why my grandma said that acting was only a game, and for a girl from an ordinary home maybe it is not a smooth career. I sometimes wonder how my own life would have turned out if I had been chosen to be a film star. Would I be happier than I am now? Who knows?

## *How Tired These Children Are !*

Before I chatted with Zhou Yiwei, I always wanted to find out what those parents thought about, who sent their children to study acting and become stars of stage and screen.

The curiosity originated from my own experience. In the winter of 2003 I had a chance to act as "An Dun" in a movie. One of the characters was a five-year-old boy sent by an agency. We started for the set before dawn. In our car was the boy, accompanied by his father. I learned that the boy would earn about 70 yuan a day. The agency would take 20 yuan as its fee. I also learned that some unscrupulous agencies offered only 50 yuan a day, and would take half of that as their fee. I told the deputy director of the film company that I would never let a child of mine do such work, but she assured me that plenty of parents were eager to get their children's names known to movie directors, even if it meant their working gratis. Their motto was: "The earlier the better!"

In the course of shooting, the father of the child left. The reason was that the father's presence would inhibit the staff from directing the child, maybe even scolding him. Luckily, we didn't frighten the boy, and the scenes were shot smoothly. Nevertheless, the boy and his father had to wait until everything was finished before they could return home. By that time it was after eight o'clock in the evening, and the boy was so tired that he slept all the way home.

That day I managed to find time to chat with the father. I asked him if he was using his little boy just to earn money. He said, "It's not just to earn money." He then stopped abruptly. So I imagined that the father wanted his child to realize his own dream of being a star. There are so many actors in the world, but only a handful become stars. Is it the children who want to become stars or their parents?

I was lucky to meet Zhou Yiwei. It was only then that I understood how a child could pursue the unrealized dream of its parent. Of course, there are parents who are different from Zhou Yiwei, but they still rely on their children to bring success to the family, and such children may have to work much harder than Zhou Yiwei's daughter.

Zhou Yiwei told me that her daughter is determined to pass the entrance examination of the Beijing Film Academy. She even goes so far as to vomit up food in order to stay slim. She has also prepared a pad using medicinal herbs to lighten the skin of her face, and applies it to her face for 20 minutes before going to bed. However, I'm worried that such treatment might weaken the skin.

There are some things that Zhou Yiwei worries about. Some girls in her daughter's class are obsessed with expensive clothes, handbags, makeup and jewelry. They too are keen to act in films or TV plays, and seem to be reckless about their own reputation.

When I listened to Zhou Yiwei talking about her girlhood, I felt that her warm memories had never faded. But when she talked about her daughter, I was worried that the dream of that young girl had become tarnished; the colors did not look so bright any more. The world of the performing arts is full of temptations, and so there are infinite dangers. I hope Zhou Yiwei's daughter is lucky enough to avoid all the temptations and dangers, and gain the glory she longs for. I'm sure that this is what the parents of all such daughters wish for.

# *The Fateful Re-Encounter*

**Time of interview**: May 5, 2001

June 1, 2001

September 29, 2008

**Place**: Underground Playground of Traders' Hotel, Beijing

McDonald's in Guiyou Store, Beijing

Sheraton Hotel, Tianjin

Liu Quan, male, 47, from Beijing, with a higher-education background. He used to own a software development company. Later, he closed his company to take care of his mentally disabled son. From then on, he was a professional stock trader without a formal job.

Yang Aili, female, 44, from Tianjin, with a higher-education background. She used to be a PE teacher in a high school in Beijing. In 1996, after her divorce, she went to Australia. There she worked as a cleaning woman and later saleswoman, and at the same time she is qualified as a teacher at a health center for handicapped children.

In 2004 Yang Aili came back to China, and began to take care of her handicapped son together with his father Liu Quan. At Spring Festival 2006, she and Liu Quan held their second wedding ceremony. On October 18, 2008, they went to Australia to live.

Liu Quan: I went all out to make money, and spent as much time as possible to take care of and be with him. If one day in the future we have to leave each other, at least he will be able to use the money his dad made for him to pay for care in a welfare home. That way he wouldn't be a burden on anyone or on the country.

Life is composed of many unexpected things. Maybe it's the so many unexpected things that make life so interesting and meaningful.

When I was young I used to mock and laugh at the mentally disabled children that I saw in my residential area. But I didn't expect that one day my son would also be mentally disabled, just like them, would also face a fate of being mocked by his peers, and would become a burden on society one day.

When my wife was pregnant I had just established my own company, so I was very busy. My wife was a PE teacher in a high school. When she had been pregnant for eight months, one very windy day I was supposed to pick her up, but a client was visiting my company, so I grudged leaving. I let her take a taxi home. She didn't, but walked. She thought it was unnecessary to spend the 10-yuan fare because our home is just on the other side of a railway from her school. As a result, she slipped and fell when crossing railway line.

She underwent many examinations in a hospital. All the doctors said the baby was all right. When the child was almost two years old we felt something was wrong. He grew too slowly, couldn't focus his eyes on one point and couldn't speak. Finally, we realized that he was handicapped, and according to the doctor, the injury to his brain in the womb was severe, so there was only a slim chance of recovery.

Maybe from that day on, my wife and I both fell into a state of great remorse. We dared not recall that windy day, and then we blamed ourselves. The remorse was really severe torture, so severe that we could barely face each other. Then about a year later my wife suggested a divorce, and offered to take the child.

Even now I dare say we loved each other very much. Neither of us has remarried since the divorce many years ago. She shouldn't support the child. I am a man, and a man is born to solve problems that women can't solve. Another reason is that I also thought that it was my fault, just like she thought it was her fault. If I had picked her up, everything would have been fine.

We finally divorced, but I kept the child. Soon after divorce she went abroad, maybe because she was too sad. Every year she posted the child some money. As far as I know, she never had a boyfriend.

For several generations my family had only one child. That means if I don't remarry and have a baby my family will become extinct. But I didn't want to remarry, because I still loved my wife and I was worried about our child. Even if another woman loved me, could she treat the child the same way she treated me? Even if she would treat him with love at first, could she continue when she had her own baby? So I didn't want to bother others but myself. Since that was my fate, I had to bear it.

Because I was too stubborn, my parents refused to take care of the child for me. It was depressing, but I don't want to blame them. I just felt it was unjust. The child was innocent, and his fate was pre-decided by adults, but he had to face indifference and disfavor, and even his relatives regarded him as a burden and couldn't accept him. Thinking of this, I would feel he was lucky, for he couldn't understand or feel the dislike; otherwise how badly hurt he would be?

As time went by, I got used to this situation. The child couldn't speak well, but I don't think he has no ideas or feelings at all. We are together day and night, and we have our own communication method. When I was operating my company, I took him to work every day. He got up early. He couldn't tell the time, but he could sense the time to wake me up. Sometimes before I woke up, he sat on the side of the bed with his eyes closed as if he was thinking of questions. Whenever I looked at him stealthily he would realize it. Then he would drag my arms and say, "Up!" I felt he had established a regular routine—he would go out at the same time every day, including Saturday and Sunday. If I didn't take him out, he would ask me to take him for a walk by repeatedly saying, "Go," and then he would calm down when we were back. I think I am a good child protector. I never failed to meet his requirements, and his requirements were originally less than other children's. It is wrong to hurt a child, a child who doesn't know what affection is or warm clothes and plenty of food, even if you know he has no IQ.

It is very hard for a man to take care of a child who mustn't be left alone for one moment. But I had no choice, and the child has a right to live. I think he definitely knows this, and, given a chance, he would never choose his existing condition.

It was an incidental thing that made me determined to close my company and devote myself to the child. It was early in 2000, a snowy winter day. I went out to buy something. I left the child at home for I didn't want him to go out with me. He had toys. I knew he didn't know how to play with them, but I still bought him a lot. Maybe it was my state of mind that I always took him as a normal child spontaneously, or you can call it self-deception, or a beautiful dream. Among those toys his favorite was a plastic inflatable seal, which he took wherever he went. So I passed him the seal and told him: "Dad is going to buy you some nice food. Wait for me at home." He gave no reaction, as usual. I wanted to come back as soon as possible. But when I was back, I saw him holding the seal standing in the corridor. He was pressing his head against the handrail and hitting it with his chin. That was the first time that I saw fear in his eyes. I thought something was wrong, so I ran towards him. Unexpectedly he grabbed my hand, and spoke a word: "Scared."

I felt my heart almost break.

Then I made the decision to close the company. I was already over 40, and didn't want to be a small boss. I couldn't forget the past, when I had hurt my son and lost my family just because of a client.

What is the freest and most profitable career? After thinking it over, I decided to be a stock trader. My economic status was all right, and I could be listed as average. My work place was a room filled with several people like me, and I could take the child there with me. He knew nothing about stocks, but whenever I watched the major stock indices he would watch them with me very seriously. Sometimes they teased him by asking him whether the indices had

risen or dropped. After thinking a little while my son would answer "Risen!"
That's the only word he could say, and because of this word, my co-workers all
liked him very much. They called him Lucky Star.

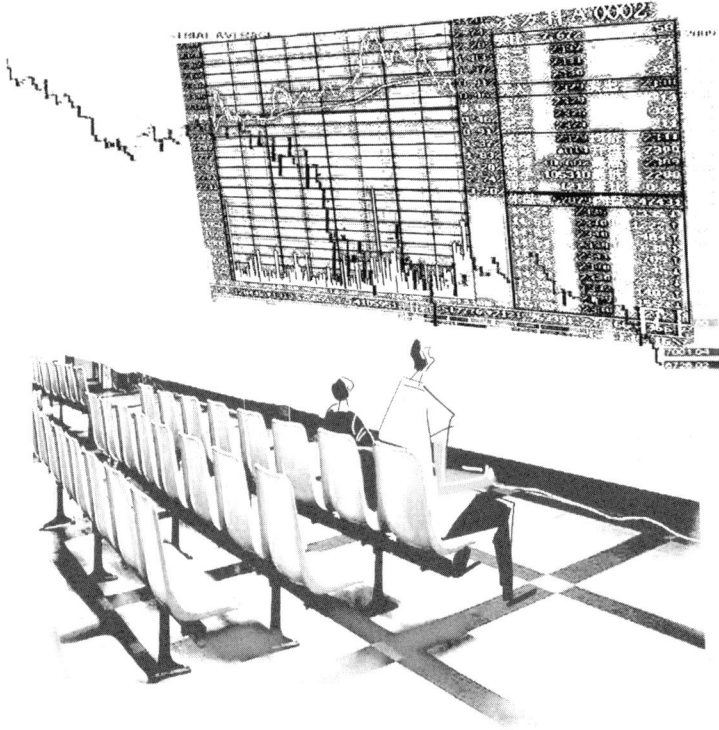

I never treat my son unfairly. Every holiday or weekend I take him for
dinner or to a playground. He is very sensible. Sometimes if I take him to a
fancy hotel for dinner he will turn around to leave at once. When I pull him
back he will say a word after a long while: "Expensive."

There are too many such things, and because of this I think he is becoming
smarter and smarter. I know I'm comforting myself, but which parents don't
cherish their own children as treasures? In this sense, there's no difference
between normal children and disabled children.

Maybe I'm getting old, but sometimes I am really very sentimental. I
often think: Now I'm able to take care of him and we can depend on each

other. But what if some day I can't do this any more? When I walk in a street seeing cars passing by me quickly, I often think: What if I suffer an unforeseen disaster?

I go all out to make money and spend as much time as possible to take care of and be with him. If one day in the future we have to leave each other, at least he can use money his dad has made for him to pay for care in a welfare home. That way he wouldn't become a burden on anyone or on the country.

The doctor says such a child won't live long. I am not afraid to see him die before me. If I can bring him as much joy as possible when he is alive, I would rather see him die first. This way he wouldn't become a burden on society or get hurt, and his life would be perfect.

Yang Aili: We could get back together after so many years because we know we can't live without each other and our son can't live without us. Maybe it's our family's fate.

It's a pity you were not present at our wedding. When we got married the first time, I was not so excited, and had not so many complicated feelings and thoughts. At over 20 years old, I married this man from Beijing. He thought he mustn't fail my parents, so he came to my hometown and held a wedding ceremony and took me away. It was very decent, for he met all my parents' requirements in all aspects, including the banquet, gifts for friends, new clothes and jewelry and a crazy carnival. From then on, he was my father's son-in-law, my husband and my child's father. That was my simple feeling at that time.

But this time it was different. He came to my parents' again. My parents were already too old for any marriage rituals. "A meal is all right," they said. "You two were originally husband and wife, and parents of a handicapped child. So forget the rituals." I told this to Liu Quan. "Fine," he said, "But we must wear new clothes, and I'll buy you a ring. The wedding ceremony is not necessary. We'll have lots of pictures taken of us in our new clothes, and show them to our son." I said it was useless for he wouldn't understand what it was all about. "Yes, he will understand after he has looked at them time and again," Liu Quan said.

You know our son is mentally retarded. We divorced for the sake of him. I didn't want to, but I really thought I should go away at that time. He is our only son, but he is mentally retarded. This means my husband won't have descendants. I said I would take the child, and let him marry another woman, who could bear a normal child. Liu Quan said times were different, and he insisted that it was he who was responsible for the child's handicap. When I was pregnant I slipped and fell down one day. He had promised to drive me home, but he didn't because he had a visiting client. I didn't take a taxi for I wanted to save money. All this ruined the baby. From that day on, when we realized our son's flaw, we kept criticizing ourselves. Finally we both wanted to divorce. I wanted him to marry a woman who could give him a baby, and he wanted me to marry a man to live a comfortable life and end the life of torture with him and the child. But after all, we love and think much about each other.

Perhaps Liu Quan concealed something from you. He was very rude then. He forced me to leave, and cried every day. He often said, "Go! If you don't go, I can't live. I feel guilty at the sight of you. I owe you and our son a lot. Go and find another man. Even if you don't give birth again, at least you needn't face your disabled son. Just go." I often wcep whenever I think of this. At the time I regretted having met a man like him. He made me feel he really wanted me to leave so he could marry another woman. In fact he hated me, though he was unwilling to blame me. One minute I would think he was a kind man and the next minute I would think he was ambushing me. Honestly, I really couldn't face my child. He is miserable, a two-year-old boy forever.

Our conflict lasted until we couldn't bear it any longer. Finally I said, "I'm leaving. Let me take him to find a home with my older brother in Australia."

"No," Liu Quan said, "He is my son. Nobody can take him. If you married another man, he would hate my son, and kill him." The process of our mutual torturing was too painful. We used every method we could, and almost drove each other crazy. We were almost dead. On our divorce day we both wept.

"Let's have a drink," he said. That was the first and only time that I got drunk. After drinking a pot of rice wine, we cried again.

"Thank you," he said, "Our divorce agreement relieves me. Don't worry about our son, and never come back." I said, "Liu Quan, there is only one goal in my future life, i. e. , to make money for our son. If one day I get sick and die, and our son is left alone, you can send him to a welfare home with the money and ask them to look after him."

I went to Australia less than a year after the divorce. Before leaving, I visited them. Liu Quan was thinner, but he said, "Look at you! You're more like a shadow than a person." After the divorce I went back to my parents' in Tianjin. My parents didn't blame me, but Mum often wept. "Dad and I are both healthy. If Liu Quan gets married again, you can bring your son here. A step-mother can't love her step-son. What's more, the child isn't clever, and if he is abused, he won't be able to complain." She wept every time she said this. At that time I got ill and went to hospital. I was diagnosed with autonomic nervous disorder. Mum felt things couldn't get any worse, so she wrote to my elder brother, asking him to come back. "If she continues like this, she will go crazy or die," she told him.

Life was really hopeless then. I thought over and over about what I could do for my son. I was a PE teacher. They say PE teachers are simple-minded but with strong limbs, and that's why Liu Quan refused to let me see the child again. What could I do? Then I decided to leave with my brother. My sister-in-law was an Australian, and she would help me there. When I arrived there, I would first learn the language while working. There's nothing I couldn't do for my son. It would be better to do that than do nothing at my parents'.

Then I went to Australia. In my thirties, I was a stranger in a strange place.

Let's get back to our topic. After going to Australia I never contacted Liu Quan. I felt that Liu Quan had forced me to get a divorce because he wanted to free me and support our son by himself, which should have been our common responsibility. Then I realized everything gradually. His relatives had abandoned him just because he refused to leave the child with me. He operated his company while taking care of our son. How hard it was for him! I knew he wouldn't get married again, for no woman would marry him. In fact he knew that if he left the child with me and continued his business, he could find another woman. But still he kept the child, because he had already made up his mind to do so. Since I knew this, I didn't think that I could love again. If I fell in love and remarried, I would be too treacherous.

Everything we did was for our son. Even now we can't tell exactly how our son became mentally retarded. If we hadn't experienced this accident, we would have a boy or a girl and bring it up, like other couples. He could do his business and I could do teaching. That way we could still be living together. And if either of us felt terrible, maybe he or I could have an affair. No big deal, for our child would already be grown up and we would be rich. That would be a very ordinary life, not worth recording. Our real life, however, was different. From the day our son was declared mentally retarded, our life was doomed to be different.

We were separated for about ten years, and, as Liu Quan told you, neither of us fell in love with anyone else. It was pathetic for us. We were both healthy and robust adults, but, just as we told each other later on, it was true that we couldn't find a new love, for at the thought of our son we just couldn't do that. I don't know whether others can understand our feelings or not. People who don't understand us might not believe it was true. Maybe they think we were deceiving each other. In Sydney I had a suitor who was fine in all aspects, and if I had responded we could have become a couple. But I just couldn't. Let me put it this way. When I walked out of the market I would see the man's car parking there, but I just couldn't walk over to him, because I felt a pair of eyes were staring at me, my son's pure and innocent eyes. I felt he was saying, "Mum, do you want another child? You don't want me any more?" At the thought of that I couldn't move in that direction at all.

I told this to Liu Quan, and he said, "So what? I would never allow anyone to share my love for my son. Though he is only a mentally retarded boy, since you left he is all I have. I spend all my time and energy on him. He is the focus of my life. "

Maybe this is parents' love for their children, and parents like us have more love for our handicapped children.

Before you came for the first time in 2001, we agreed that he would tell you more than a love story. It is a very special life for parents who have a disabled child. I met many parents of this kind abroad, and I know that feeling. That's a process of falling from Heaven into Hell, and then you look for a new Heaven. It's a torment that is indescribable.

Liu Quan suffered more than I did. It was hard for me to make money, and life was difficult, but he had to take care of a baby. As long as a man can take care of a normal child for ten years with love and patience, he is a good man, let alone a mentally retarded child. Once I asked him: "How did you live with our son? Tell me. Were you impatient or did you ever want to give up?"

He replied, "Sometimes I was tired and sometimes I felt desperate, but I never wanted to give up, because if his parents give him up, he will die. " I cried at his words. We experienced all those things, and now so many years have passed, but if we started over, everything would still be very hard for us.

So I never asked Liu Quan to recall anything. "You needn't tell me how hard it was for you. I can imagine. You are the father who suffers most in the world. Compared with you, I'm not a good mother. Let me pay you back in the future. You love me by loving our son, I know. " I said.

Let me talk about my experiences abroad. I'm not complaining, for I'm not eligible to complain compared with Liu Quan. I just want to tell you the feelings of parents like us.

I was a PE teacher. I never liked academic study. I married Liu Quan, which meant a comfortable life for me, so I became lazier. My English was originally poor, and after marriage and giving birth to the baby and divorce, my English was almost gone. So I was almost helpless abroad.

I'm very grateful to my brother and sister-in-law. My sister-in-law is a doctor. She is very kind. My brother told her everything about my situation, and she had great sympathy for me. She asked me to live with them, and found me a language school to solve my language problem first.

Maybe there's one more thing Liu Quan hasn't told you. When we divorced, he gave me two-thirds of our common savings. I took US $ 2,000 abroad, and had my mum send the rest to my husband and son. "You two love each other. Why divorce? It'll be all right if you have another baby. You have no genetic problem," Mum said. I didn't explain, for I didn't think she could understand, and an outsider would never understand our feelings about what we owed each other. Honestly, we dared not have another baby, for we didn't want another tragedy. And we didn't want to see a normal child grab the love my son could have owned. Birds of a feather flock together. Liu Quan and I are the same kind of people; otherwise things would be different now.

I lived in my brother's house, and gave my sister-in-law US $ 1,000. "This is for my living expenses and language school tuition. You arrange these for me, and when I can speak English, I'll find a job," I told my sister-in-law. She took the money, and said, "Living expenses are not necessary. You just need to pay your tuition fee." Then I applied to a nearby language school whose specialty is giving language training to Chinese.

I think I'm diligent. I knew I couldn't go back to Tianjin for the time being, and I didn't want to go back at once, so I had to support myself. Besides, I had a son in China who could never support himself. Due to my son's mental deficiency, what I feared most was death. As long as I'm alive, I can look after him at any time. I missed the two of them very much then, and I thought, "Liu Quan, take care. It's our son's luck that we are both alive." Nobody wanted him to be rich more than I did in the whole world. I didn't want his money, but if he got rich, my son's life could be guaranteed.

Thinking of these things, I devoted myself to study, and carried notes around with me all the time—even in the bathroom. My brother said he had never seen me work so hard, and he didn't know I was so intelligent. Within less than half a year I could already chat with others and take care of myself.

Then my brother said: "You must choose a regular school to study in. You are not qualified to work right now, as your visa isn't the right kind." So I began to consider what kind of work I should do as my life career. Dreams are often related to life conditions. I had a mentally retarded son, so my dream was related to him. There are such families, such children and such parents like us in every corner of the world, and in Sydney too. I thought a major related to infant education and mentally retarded children would be useful whether I stayed at home or abroad, and my own son would benefit from it.

My brother is the child's uncle. He said he didn't agree. At the time he was studying for his doctor's degree. Hearing my words, he wept. "Aili, you are stupid," he said. "Why did Liu Quan force you to leave your child? He just wanted you to get rid of pain. Now you want to learn this, which means you must face families and children like your own. How could you stand it?"

"I've made up my mind," I replied. "I will learn this. Even if I can't help others, at least I can help my son. Whenever conditions permit, I will bring him to me."

"You will find no relief all your life," my brother said. I thought, "If you had such a child you would find no relief either, unless you were cruel, emotionless and irresponsible. Once you got such a child, your life would be rewritten. He would be the worry, pain and fear of your life as long as you loved him."

Studying was hard for me because I had to work to support myself. Though my brother and sister-in-law offered to support me, I couldn't allow myself to accept their good will. I wasn't able to enter a famous university, and besides, I didn't have enough money. At last I chose a course in infant psychology and life coaching. You need to take an exam to get a professional certificate, just like Chinese junior college education.

I began to work once my studies started. At first I was a cleaner, similar to part-time servants who clean others' houses. Because my sister-in-law was a native, I was accepted by an agency and got many jobs. We had uniforms and cleaning tools, and we were sent to clients' houses at appointed times. We got payment from our clients, and the clients settled their accounts directly with our company. At first my sister-in-law didn't believe I was willing to do this. When I told her I saw the recruitment ads and wanted her to be my guarantor, she was surprised. "How can you do this? Your brother says you never did anything at home," she said.

"I can do it. I must support myself and pay tuition, and make money for my son. I'm willing to do any work I can do. "

I led a very simple existence as a cleaner. Every day I worked and studied. Take working as an example. I really never worked at home, but times had changed. I had to clean the dirtiest corners in others' houses at their command. The last procedure was floor mopping. For quite a long time that was the hardest moment for me. It reminded me I was a cleaner. Frankly, whatever my life is in China, I would never think of doing this. But one has to adapt to different conditions, and when I made money for myself and my son, I would feel my work wasn't that bad. It was labor, and labor is the most glorious thing.

During my cleaning days I found a new field of endeavor: I could knit sweaters. Foreigners like individualized and hand-made sweaters. An old lady liked a sweater I had brought from China, and she asked whether I could knit her one. I told her to give me yarn and promised to knit her one. We didn't discuss money. During my time cleaning her house she was very kind to me. We were already friends, so I made the sweater as a favor. When I had finished it, she was very happy. A few days after that she said one of her friends wanted one too. She urged me to accept money for it. So I began to knit another sweater. Before I finished it I got new orders from her neighbors and friends. The old lady told them about my background and my son. She told them I was an ingenious and good Chinese mother, and unexpectedly she set a price for my work without my permission. She went to my company and asked whether I could work in her house every day. I was for it, and so was the company. It was good because I could get a regular income. The old lady was very lovely. "Come to my house every day and knit sweaters for us," she said. "We'll learn from you. "

That was a very happy period for me. Every day I went to her house on time to meet her and her friends. I knitted sweaters with them, and they learnt from me. What I knitted was sweaters on the orders that the old lady got for me. I really hadn't expected that knitting sweaters could make me money. I can't remember how many sweaters I knitted in those days.

In the fourth year after I went abroad I got help from a family for whom I had done cleaning work. A market the man of the family had invested in opened, and he asked whether I wanted to be a saleswoman there. "Maybe it's beyond me," I said. "Since you can take others' houses as your own and clean them, you can do anything," he said. I decided to try. Then I became a saleswoman. It was more tiring than cleaning, but I got more money. Besides, I had to prepare for the coming exam, so my energy and strength were almost exhausted. Though I took the exam only to get a nursery governess's certificate, it was in fact very difficult, especially for an alien like me who didn't know much about their traditions, laws and ethics, and who had only just passed a language exam. Given that I had to work to support myself and couldn't concentrate on one thing, it was even harder for me. I wanted to give up many times, but when I thought of my son I regained my confidence. As my life was getting better, I got an idea. I hoped that some day I would take my son abroad. A new environment and new way of life might inspire his intelligence and work a miracle.

I was an alien, so I could only work as a trainee in the handicapped children's center, and my salary was relatively low. But it was better than being a saleswoman. Every time I was in contact with the handicapped children and their families I would miss my son and Liu Quan. Really, I missed Liu Quan, too, even though we were no longer husband and wife. I knew he supported our child on his own and had closed his company and became a professional stock trader to take care of our son. This information made me more worried about them.

I met some experts in this field abroad. Some of them thought children like my son were not impossible to cure, and with the right coaching method they might acquire basic life skills. You know, parents of such children are happy to hear this, even if it has no scientific basis. I think it's their wish that one day a miracle might happen to their children. I hope it may happen to my son, too.

The real factor that prompted me to go back and find my husband and son was a woman who also had a mentally retarded child. She took her child to the recovery center for behavior coaching. She was very patient with her child, and she was very beautiful. Everybody there knew them. They told me she used to be an investment manager of a commercial bank, and did her job very well, but she resigned when she had the baby, and moved to the suburbs to take care of the child. I tried chatting with her. She was easy-going. Gradually I told her my son was also handicapped, and he was in China with my ex-husband, and then I told her more about my experiences. At first she only listened without responding. When I finished one day, she entrusted her child to a coach and came to chat with me. Very seriously she said, "I've thought many times what I should tell you. I think it's time for you to go home. A mother can't leave her child, especially a handicapped child who needs his mother more than other children. Nobody can replace his mother. Maybe your absence will deprive him of a chance of recovery. Only his mother can be his best doctor and friend. Is there a better career waiting for you apart from him? Does anyone in the world need you more than he does? I think you should do for your child what you are doing for others' children. "

Maybe to make a life choice only takes one minute. I thought her words over and over that day, and read the online story you wrote about my husband and son again and again. I thought I should go home. Suddenly I felt that life had shown me a very ridiculous aspect of myself: As a mother, why couldn't I face my own son?

In autumn 2004 I went back to Tianjin. I left my stuff at my parents' home, and went directly to Beijing. I knew Liu Quan was still living in our old house with my son. He grudged buying a new house. Once he told my mother: "The child and I don't need a big house, so save the money for his future. "

Nobody was home. I made a phone call to Liu Quan. At the sound of my voice, he asked: "What's wrong?" Tears fell at once from my eyes. His voice was very thoughtful, as if he could come over to solve my problem at once. Many years before, whenever I called him his first words were also "What's wrong?"

"I'm back," I said, "I am at the door of our house. " He was wordless for a while, and then said, "We're in the community hospital. Our son has caught a cold. "

"I'm coming right away," I said.

I reencountered my son in the community hospital. I don't want to depict the scene, otherwise I would cry. My son was grown up, and my husband seemed a little old. They were expressionless at the sight of me. Now I think being expressionless is normal. What expression does it need? We are a family. It was just like I was there just to give them something, nothing special. My son was on a drip. Liu Quan stood up. There were newspapers and bottles on the chair beside him. It was very dismal.

I reached out my hands to catch my son's, and he didn't refuse. He stared at me and then at Liu Quan, as if he knew me. Liu Quan told my son very softly: "She's your mother." My son smiled. His teeth were white and perfect.

I stood there in tears. Liu Quan reached out his arms. I felt he wanted to hug me but he was hesitating. I leaned in his arms and said: "I'll wait for you two to go home together." His beard scratched my face. I never knew he had such hard bristles before.

We ate outside that day. Liu Quan said there was no time to cook, and our son was hungry. Liu Quan took us to a lamb hot-pot restaurant nearby. "In Australia they don't eat this stuff, right?" he asked. On our way, I took my son's hand, and very happily he followed me and repeated again and again: "Mum, mum, mum." I couldn't control my tears. Oh, my little stupid boy. I felt he knew me and knew I was his mum so he was happy, smiling and eating like a horse. His movements were a little clumsy, but he needed no help.

After the meal, Liu Quan asked me: "Where are you staying?"

"Nowhere yet. Can I stay at your place?" I asked. He agreed.

I think if a couple without children divorce they would never want to meet again unless they don't really want to divorce. But this isn't the case with a couple having children, for there's something untold existing forever between them, and their children connect the two of them forever, believe it or not.

I cried again at the sight of their house. I cried because they were living so well. How could Liu Quan make their house so tidy and comfortable! That night we ate at home. Liu Quan said, "Let me make noodles for you, and our son will help me. " He made the dough, and my son sat on a bench preparing the vegetables. When he saw that his dad's dough was ready, he stood up and fetched the chopping board. Liu Quan said, "Though he can't speak, he knows what to do very well. Later on, when I boil the noodles he will fetch the bowls. " Just think, how many times it would take to cry out all my tears? I just stood there and cried on and on, and all of a sudden, Liu Quan's tears dropped onto the dough.

Neither of us started a love conversation until we decided to resume our marriage. From that day on I began to live in Beijing, and we never asked about whether there was a love affair during those years.

We stayed together for our first night not as a couple but as old friends. "I have an idea. Let's emigrate and take our son abroad for recovery treatment. There may be a miracle," I said.

"I have thought about this before," he said, "but I'm afraid I couldn't make enough money to give a good life to our son. "

We continued our chat like this. I talked about what I had seen and heard abroad, and he talked about how he had invested in stocks, and then we fell asleep during our conversation. The next morning our son woke me up. He dragged Liu Quan's arm and said, "Up!" and we two awoke in confusion. I thought to myself: "Yang Aili, that's the blueprint for the rest of your life. "

In fact without the idea of emigration we wouldn't have had to remarry. We could get back together after so many years because we knew we couldn't live without each other and our son couldn't live without us. Maybe it's our family's fate.

Liu Quan had been trading stocks. When the stock market was prosperous years ago, he made some money. Now we haven't bought a new house or car. We are busy with our emigration qualifications because we still hope maybe our son could wake up in another environment, in a different life style, or with another type of therapy. This is our dream, and an expectation deepest in our hearts. We will never give up, however silly the dream is. It includes many factors like maternal love, paternal love, and so on, and also a factor nobody wants to point out directly, i. e. we are both worried that if we become old and

die our son would be left alone. I believe that's the biggest worry of all parents like us, and people without our experience can hardly understand it.

*The Passage of Seven Years*

When I met Liu Quan in 2001, he was a single father with a mentally retarded son. He was a professional stock trader. He took his son to work. He was both father and mother.

Once I heard about the story of Liu Quan and his son, I couldn't forget it. Different people had different reactions to the details of the story when they heard them. After a long period of silence, a lady of about 40 asked me: "In real life, who are more willing to sacrifice? Men or women?" I just couldn't figure out an answer.

The interview comprised two parts and was finished in two different places. It was a long interview, because during our interview the child often blurted out such words as "thirsty" or "shu" (which means to pee). At such times Liu Quan would meet the child's requirements before he finished apologizing to me. Frankly speaking, the child wasn't easy to take care of, but there was no any touch of impatience in Liu Quan's movements or expression.

Sometimes from his patience I even perceived a man's purity and tenderness toward children.

And it was at that time that I knew there was a knot that couldn't be untied. He thought he was responsible for his son's injury in the womb and his disability. He thought he had failed his son and his wife. He supported the child on his own for the sake of not only paternal love but compensation.

I was so touched by Liu Quan during the one-year interview that I was soaked with tears. When he said he would leave the child some money in order that he wouldn't become a burden on society, I was touched even more. I thought: Just by looking at him you will know how a man loves his children.

Then when I finished *A Single Man and His Mentally Retarded Son* many readers wrote to me. Among them were some women readers who conveyed their wish to take care of the two of them. I thought that was very kind, so I passed those letters on to Liu Quan. Liu Quan took them, but from the women readers' complaint I knew he didn't write a single word to them. I asked him why, and he said he didn't want to entangle anyone. "No. You are waiting for your ex-wife," I said.

"As long as she doesn't remarry, I can't seek another woman," he replied.

"Maybe she has already remarried, and she hasn't told you yet because she doesn't want to hurt you," I said, "Otherwise, why hasn't she come back?"

He got angry: "Nonsense! You don't know what's going on between us."

Then I apologized and said, "I didn't mean it. I said it to get you to tell me what's going on between you two. You love each other. Just wait. Re-encounter causes lovers sorrow. When you get together again in tears don't forget to buy me a drink." It took me seven years to see that day come.

Liu Quan invited me to go to Tianjin one day. He said he wanted to introduce me a person named Yang Aili. That was the first time I had heard this name. "Is that your ex-wife?" I asked. "No. It's my wife, mother of my son," he declared with a smile.

Maybe it surprised many, but not me. I strongly believed and knew that that day would come, right from a year before, when I got to know Liu Quan and his story, I knew it would come. "You're not a good journalist, because you estimate things with your instinct." Liu Quan said with a smile.

"All right. Just take it as a dream that lasted seven years," I replied.

We decided to meet in Tianjin. I chose the place. "My son would leave and say it's expensive again." Liu Quan said.

"Which is the most expensive hotel in Tianjin?" I asked. "I'll treat you. I want to treat you to the fanciest place as long as I can afford it, no matter whether the food is tasty or not. Thank you for fulfilling my dream, though the dream often makes me cry."

On September 29, for the first time I met Liu Quan's ex-wife, who had become his wife for the second time.

You would want to make friends with the easy-going woman, only because of her talking style. Her tolerance is not made up, but is from her heart. Yang Aili was wearing a long shirt with the sleeves rolled up, and the cuffs clipped with pins. She reached out her hand, and gave me a strong handshake. Her hand was big, hard and warm. Then she laughed. "I'm a working woman, as you can tell from my hands," she said. I didn't pay much attention to her hands until later, when she narrated her cleaning experience, and said, "Labor is glorious" in the interview. I estimated that before she went abroad and worked there she had taken good care of her hands.

After we sat down, Liu Quan triggered our conversation. He said, "We are leaving for Australia with our son soon. After thinking it over and over again we decided that we should do something and meet some people." They had thought of me. They had reached an agreement that Yang Aili would be the narrator, for Liu Quan had had no experience abroad. He said, "In your presence, maybe she can't conceal anything from me. I know it was hard for her." While he was saying this, Yang Aili put her hand on the back of his, patted it, and said: "Don't think this way. Neither of us lived in comfort."

They were talking sweet nothings while I was admiring them. Sometimes hardships make miracles. They were burdened with troubles, but they were writing a more beautiful life story.

This time Liu Quan was only a listener. He passed me a tissue every time

I cried, and when a packet of tissues had been used up he went to buy another one. Taking the chance of his absence, his wife told me that no one was more suitable to be a father and husband than he was. While saying this, she smiled through her tears. Her expression was very complicated.

We had a lavish meal that day. The whole table was taken up with delicious food, both Chinese and Western. We couldn't eat it all, so I asked Liu Quan to take the remainder with him. Yang Aili said: "Look, you are not treating us. What's this? My son says it could only be called a muddle and a mess."

"Do me a favor." I said, "The muddle and mess contains the feelings that I can't express."

On my way back to Beijing from Tianjin I heard a foreigner singing the *Letter to the Corinthians* from the Bible in English. I sang with him:

"Love suffers long and is kind. Love does not envy. Love does not parade itself, is not puffed up. Bears all things, believes all things, hopes all things, endures all things. Love never fails."

I decided to give a CD of this to Liu Quan's family as a gift. They made me understand that sometimes love changes fate and illuminates lives that could have been dark.

While I was writing up this interview, I thought, "Is it a complicated story?" I don't think so. No story is complicated if we only focus on its plot instead of its emotions. A life-and-death story can be told in just a few sentences, but if emotions are added, a simple story can become complicated, and a banal story interesting, and thus we can get more understanding and inspiration.

On the night before I finalized the manuscript I was still trying to abridge the story of the family, and during this process I kind of lost my bearings. It was regrettable that I could only tell so little and had to omit many details causing me to weep time and again. I just wanted to keep as much of their feelings and thoughts as possible. After all, they are a little different from those families that separate and then get together again, thus their paths of feelings and love are doomed to be very rugged.

# For Other People Is Also for Yourself

**Time of interview**: March 5 and March 11, 2008

**Place**: Office of the Photographic Department of *Beijing Youth Daily*

Zhang Zuo is a Beijinger, male, 50 years old. After graduating from high school, he was sent to the countryside as an "educated youth," * and then returned to the city, where he once worked as a bricklayer. Later, he taught himself photography and darkroom production techniques, and was assigned to the Beijing Cultural Center in Chongwen District, to work in the darkroom. Now he is working at the *China Youth Daily* as a full-time darkroom operator. He published a book titled *Interpretation of the Hidden Shadows of Black and White— the Production and Thinking of a Darkroom Operator*. Another book of his, with the title *The Heavy Task*, was awarded the Gold Prize at the fourth Nikon National Photographic Competition.

———

\* a special term in modern Chinese history, referring to the young urban people who went to work as peasants in the countryside in the 1960s and 1970s, either voluntarily or perforce. Most of them received an incomplete junior or senior secondary education only.

## Learning photography changed my life.

I wouldn't say that I am talented. But from the time I was a little boy I had practical abilities, especially when it came to handicrafts.

I was born into a teacher's family, as the first child. When I was only eight or nine years old, I learned to do housework, such as cooking gruel, making steamed bread and baking pancakes. These can be regarded as "handicrafts", can't they? When I was a primary school student, I liked making papercuts, paper toys and kites. In middle school, I became good at lettering, and joined the blackboard newspaper. After I was sent to the countryside I was engaged in farm work. After two years, I returned to the city and worked as a bricklayer for a construction company. My life was quite simple, but I thought that I should find a more cultural pursuit. In the construction team, there was a fellow who liked to take pictures, and who had once studied in a photography class. I did not want to be a bricklayer all my life, and I believed that learning photography might bring some changes in my life. If I failed to make a living out of photography, I could still take souvenir pictures for family members, co-workers and friends. My parents agreed to my plan, and after saving up for a year, I bought a Konica 135 automatic camera, and taught myself to take pictures.

At that time when I was learning photography, I couldn't afford to buy color films. It was also very expensive to develop the films, so I began to be interested in developing and enlarging pictures. Before I could afford to buy an enlarger, I took my films to a photo studio. Again, it took me a year to save up enough money to buy the basic equipment required for a darkroom. It was only at night that I had time to enlarge pictures.

I changed my job in order to devote myself more fully to photography when I met Xie Hailong, who worked at the Beijing Cultural Center in Chongwen District. Among amateur photographers in Beijing, he enjoyed a high reputation, and he was also the tutor of amateurs like myself. With his help, I was assigned to the Beijing Cultural Center and was engaged in darkroom work.

**My destiny was decided by my character.**

At that time, many people who learned photography became press photographers later. But I am an introvert, not like them. When I was assigned to the *China Youth Daily* I continued doing darkroom work. Those who became press photographers were all braver than I. I am afraid to take pictures of people, as they might object, and cause trouble. But in the darkroom, I feel very free. It is a world of my own. I feel quite safe, happy and contented. I can turn pictures that other people have taken from small negatives into photographic works that can be appreciated by the general public. Before they enter the visual fields of others, they belong to me alone. I enjoy the process. I feel that the world of the darkroom is a wonderful one. Therefore, it is my destiny to work in this trade.

For me, the darkroom is a perfect world. Some people may think that my 20 years doing this work have been lonely ones for me, but I feel very happy in the darkroom, and forget all my troubles there. The photographs are from many places where I have no chance to go, and let me see people whom I have no chance to see. I get to know about the outside world through them. Besides, many of these works have emotions; those that have emotions have lives; and those that have lives have spirit. Like dressing up my children, I look at them this way and that, thinking how to make them prettier. Black-and-white pictures have only three colors—black, white and grey. But in my imagination I see a special and beautiful new world in them as I reconstruct the colors.

I have developed pictures for many photographers from all over China.

Many of their works have received prestigious awards. When I see those pictures in magazines, exhibitions or museums, and remember that they were developed by me, I feel very happy.

In the course of my darkroom work over so many years, I have met many master photographers. I feel very proud when they become my friends in the process of our cooperation. Some of them are world-famous, and they all appreciate my handling of their works.

### The process of emotional communication makes me very happy.

In my trade, there is a difference between low standard and high standard. The low standard is when one has mastered the necessary darkroom techniques, and can produce pictures according to the requirements of the photographers. But the high standard that I pursue also includes creative understanding as well as production according to requirements. For example, you should actively communicate with the photographer, find out his/her state of mind and ideas, and the environment at the time when the pictures were taken, the themes the photographer wanted to express, the key points emphasized and the information being transferred by the pictures. This is a process of emotional communication. In the process, a feeling of friendship arises between me and the photographer. I can further understand what kind of feeling there is among the photographer and the stories, figures and landscapes captured. After that, I know what I should do to make the pictures come out right. Therefore, most of the time I make friends with the photographer. I like to ponder the characters, behaviors and styles of creation. This requires more effort, but I think it is quite worthwhile. At the same time, it improves my tastes and techniques.

I have worked in this way for many years. I have made friends with many people, and we have a tacit mutual understanding. They bring their works to me without putting forward any requirements; they just tell me for what purpose the pictures will be used—for books or magazines, for an exhibition, for auction or collection. Then I know what effect the pictures should convey. In my mind, I have a file of various styles for a large number of my photographer clients, so that I can make the pictures basically fit the unspoken requirements.

Let me give you two examples.

The couple Xu Xiaobing and Hou Bo were famous revolutionary photographers in China. Their classic works with the titles, "Founding Ceremony of the PRC" and "Liberation of Nanjing" recorded part of the history of the Chinese revolution; their pictures are witnesses to history. The negatives of their pictures are all stored at Xinhua News Agency, which helped them to enlarge their pictures for exhibitions. They asked me to develop some of their negatives in 2003, the 110th anniversary of the birth of Chairman Mao, for showing at the Arles Photography Festival in France under the title "The Great Mao Zedong." The French wanted to take the negatives to France for developing, but the couple refused, insisting that I could do the job in China perfectly well. Sure enough, I met the requirements of the French side, and everybody was satisfied.

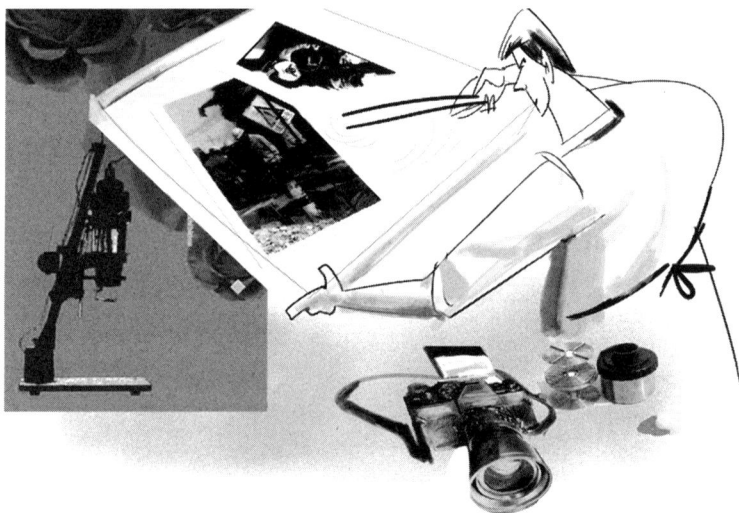

Another famous photographer, Zeng Huang, learned press photography in the US. I met him in 1995, when he was preparing to publish a collection of his photographic works with the title *Bosnia and Herzegovina*; *Living in Flames of*

*War*. He demanded that special effects must be achieved to show his personal style and reproduce the historic atmosphere of the war. My efforts did not meet with his immediate approval, and I had to do the work over and over again. He paid great attention to the tones and details. In the end, he published his book, containing a dedication to my darkroom work. His understanding of photography and his pursuit of perfection made me admire him very much.

Can you understand what I mean when I say, "For other people is also for yourself"? What I want to say is that when you work for others you can learn a lot. Everyone has his or her own advantages; every photographer has his or her unique way to observe society and express life. In the course of working for them, I also observe society and understand life from their points of view.

## Interviewer's Notes

### "The King of Black and White" and His Pure World

In a corner of the Photography Department of *China Youth Daily*, there is an obscure revolving door. Behind it is a world that belongs to Zhang Zuo, the 50-year-old darkroom master.

Zhang Zuo's treasures fill the room. They are shabby bottles and jars, bags that seem to be filled with flour, a pair of scales and a blow-dryer. In fact, the stuff in the "flour bags" is not flour, but the "solution" used for developing films. The containers are used to hold the solution, the mixing of which differs according to the nature of the picture to be developed.

Zhang Zuo's techniques ensure that the results always exceed the requirements and expectations of the photographers; even the photographers themselves are sometimes amazed to find that there is more in their pictures than they thought they saw.

In my interviews I have met two types of awkward people. One is very good at dealing with the media, very talkative and a user of fine words specially prepared for reporters, no matter how tricky the questions are. The second type dislikes talking about personal matters, but can wax eloquent when talking about others. Zhang Zuo belongs to the latter category, and this made my interview rather difficult.

I had prepared for the interview for more than two months. I had read his book *Interpretation of the Hidden Shadows of Black and White—the Production and Thinking of a Darkroom Master*. I sent questions to him by e-mail. However, the planned interview became a casual chat.

I spent two unforgettable mornings on the interview. On March 5, he stressed the fact that he had devoted his whole life to his darkroom work, and kept repeating "For other people is also for yourself." On the morning of March 11, I asked no questions at all, but followed him into the darkroom, and watched him develop pictures. The darkroom is only 14 or 15 square meters. On one side is the enlarger, and on the other side is the water tank. There are three enamel basins with solution in them. The negatives are placed in the three basins in turn, emerging from the third basin as real pictures. Zhang Zuo handles the negatives tenderly, as if they were like children being born.

One week after I interviewed Zhang Zuo, I found four photographers who had worked with him. They all praised his straightforwardness and unique skill. I couldn't help thinking when I wrote the article that one day someone should hold an exhibition of Zhang Zuo's work. Surely, his darkroom efforts have contributed as much to the modern art of photography in China as the photographers themselves!

## Appendix: Photographers talking about a darkroom maker—Zhang Zuo in the eyes of his friends

**Xie Hailong:** general secretary of the China Photographers Association

I have been acquainted with Zhang Zuo for more than 20 years. My first impression was that he was straightforward, honest and kind. Many people in photographic circles have become good friends with him. He is not good at words, but he is always willing to help others.

The relationship between a photographer and a developer can be described as brotherly affection from the points of view of both work and emotion.

From 1986 up to now, Zhang Zuo has been my personal assistant in darkroom work. He has developed pictures for me for free for more than 20 years. Many people cannot understand it. But we ourselves know that it is a feeling that our hearts have been linked, and that kind of feeling is hard to find in others. We have no monetary relationship at all; it is a complete mutual affection like friends and brothers, and this kind of trust is especially hard to find. Many years ago, when I began to shoot pictures of the Hope Project, I would stay in mountainous areas for one or two months at a time. When I returned, I handed my films over to him, because I knew he would not let me down. For so many years, he has never made any mistakes. He has always been conscientious and meticulous. For a photographer, the negatives are the most important things. Many photographers store their most treasured negatives in bank deposit boxes for safety. I have never done so; I've handed all my negatives to Zhang Zuo. I have such confidence in him!

I remember that in April 1992 my Hope Project photographic series was published in the media. For it, Zhang Zuo and I worked on more than 1,000 pictures. For a whole week, we stayed up late, and he had no complaints. When the pictures made a big stir at that time, did he gain anything? Who knew him? But he still strove for perfection, being even more earnest than I was, as if it were his series. During these years, Zhang Zuo was my first audience, every time when I returned from mountainous areas and the countryside, the first person I had to see was Zhang. There is a story only we two and the person concerned know. I once took a picture of a girl in Luanping County, Hebei Province. She was studying in a hovel, warming her frozen hands at a small fire from time to time to enable her to go on writing. I told Zhang about her, explaining that her family was too poor to send her to school. He asked me for the address and the name of the girl. The next time I saw the girl she asked me to thank "Uncle Zhang Zuo" for sending her money every month so that she could go to school again. Zhang Zuo says he is going to send her money until she graduates from college.

If you make friends with someone, you should not only be concerned about whether he treats you well or not, you should also see how he treats others and his parents. Zhang Zuo is a very filial son to his parents, and this means that he is basically a good person. When he makes friends with others, he is sincere. He is not good at saying fine words, but if he works for you, he will never try to gain an advantage by trickery. There is one thing that most people don't know about—Zhang Zuo is especially good at making portraits of the deceased, and he has done it for free for thousands of people.

Zhang Zuo also has shortcomings. His way of thinking is rigid, and he has a fancy for traditional things. This is my opinion of him. In these digital times, I once urged him to catch up with the trend. But he said that he couldn't. He said that people like him are becoming fewer and fewer. In photographic circles, there would always be someone who needed his help, and he felt happy about this. Besides, the work of the darkroom is not easy to master, he said, so it was better not to be distracted.

**Zhu Xianmin**: vice-chairman of the China Photographers Association

Darkroom work is the process of completing and perfecting an artistic creation. In fact, darkroom processing is as important as taking the pictures themselves. Photographers say that 70 percent of the success of a picture is due to the darkroom operators. So it is unfair, I think that the first reaction to a photograph is that "It is taken so well," and not "It is so well made." We only know the names of the photographers, and not those of the people who work behind the scenes to make photographs works of art.

Some people think that with the development of digital science and related technologies, it is not worth learning the craft of the darkroom, and Zhang Zuo will soon be a representative of an archaic handicraft industry.

But a good darkroom worker should be good at taking and appreciating pictures himself, have good aesthetic taste and much experience, knowledge and understanding of real life. At the same time, he should have good endurance and the ability for scientific implementation. Zhang Zuo possesses all these qualities. At the same time, he is a very honest and kind person who is trustworthy and responsible.

Many years ago, I saw some of Zhang Zuo's photographic works. I can say without exaggeration that if he had taken up photography seriously he would have been one of the best.

**Jin Yongquan**: director of the Photographic Department of *China Youth Daily*

Zhang Zuo is a very honest and kind person, and also a man full of "contradictions." For example, for reasons of the times and history, he didn't receive formal higher education, which has cramped his experience somewhat. But on the other hand, it has freed him from preconceived theories, so he comes closer to the essence that photography expresses.

He is a man with a flair for implementation. He often gives surprises to photographers, because sometimes our requirements are lower than his own production requirements. He can make the works exceed your imagination and expectations, and he exposes wonderful details that the photographers themselves didn't notice. He gives a picture more vitality and expressive force.

As a photographer myself, I think that it is a great pity that most photographers know little about darkroom work. It is a kind of loss for both the understanding and experience of photography. If you don't know about darkrooms, you cannot be regarded as understanding photography. But with digital technologies becoming more and more advanced, the trade of darkroom production is on the verge of extinction. Zhang Zuo's expertise is first class. At the same time, he is also a very professional and dedicated person. He has worked for 20 years silently, without any complaints. His persistence is admirable. But it is a pity that he is a fighting a lone battle. We need half a dozen more people like him.

**Huang Wen**: World Press Photo judge

Because many photographers who mainly rely on digital technologies don't know about darkroom techniques, they do not know how a proper picture is finally finished. When I studied photography in college, we still used film, and darkroom techniques were a required course. I still remember the mistakes I made in developing films for the first time. That made me understand that darkroom work is not easy. When we are attracted by a photograph, what we pay attention to is usually the name of the photographer—the darkroom technicians are anonymous. But in fact an excellent darkroom technician can create surprising visual wonders, often by highlighting neglected details. A good press photographer cannot do without the help of a good darkroom technician. Darkroom technology is basically a kind of craft, so I regard darkroom technicians as, in fact, darkroom artists. Photographic artists live in the limelight, while darkroom technicians work in darkness, creating magical visual effects for the works of the former.

In photographic circles, many people like to call Zhang Zuo "Respected Zuo." I also call him that. I have entrusted him with many of my works, some of which helped to create my reputation. His work is excellent, and he treats people very well. He is generous, honest and kind, like a kind older brother of mine. I still treasure the pictures he developed for me, as it was Zhang who made them more exquisite. Zhang Zuo is held in great esteem in photographic circles because he has excellent moral quality.

# *Loving Yourself Is Better Than Saving a Marriage*

**Time of Interview**: December 18, 2003 to October 3, 2008

**Place**: Yi Ming's home, an apartment in Chaoyang District;

The Special Contribution Department Office of *Beijing Youth Daily*;

Yu Gong Yu Po Restaurant near the East Third Ring Road, Beijing.

Yi Ming, female, 31 years old, is a Beijinger. Having graduated from a university in Beijing, majoring in economic management, she is now working in a foreign company.

**I think I still shouldn't go away. Maybe you will come back if I wait for you.**

When I got to know him, I was 21 and he was 29. At that time, his ideal was to own a Cherokee Jeep and a house. He was busy, and worked hard every day. That period of life was very happy. Seeing that he wore the clothes that I had washed and ironed for him, I felt very satisfied. The idea of becoming a strong woman disappeared at that moment. I knew that that was the life I wanted, making a warm small home for the one I loved, preparing everything for him, watching him go to work, making dinner for him in the evening, waiting for him to return home, relieving his fatigue with my love and tenderness, and waiting for him at a fixed place called home and loving him.

We planned to buy a house, and getting married. We investigated many housing projects, and at last we selected an apartment not far from my mother's home. But we had to wait until it became available. At that time, we lived in my parents' home. During the process of waiting, we turned from a man and a woman living together to legal husband and wife. His career was developing fast, and he returned home later and later, and at last he began not to return home for several days at a time. I turned from calling him every day to every three days, and then to once a week. I was quite depressed. I felt like a silly woman, I could do nothing but stay at home and wait for him, waiting for our new house to be completed, waiting for the sound of hurrying steps in the corridor to become nearer and nearer, clearer and clearer, until it stopped outside the door.

After that, our communication became less and less, and we even reached the stage of having nothing to talk about. After a small quarrel, he said to me: "We can't live together, let's get a divorce." On hearing that, I said calmly, "All right." Because I was really tired, the word "waiting" had made me quite fatigued, although he explained to me many times that he was busy arranging our future. Because today he had the chance, he must grasp it to earn more money, until he had earned the amount of money enough for him after 40 to enjoy life with me. But nobody knew what the amount was. The desire of men is always swelling—the more the better. Compared with his ideal, I was insignificant. I only came second to his career. If he had good luck, he would always have better chances in his career, and I would always have to wait. I didn't have very high material desires. I didn't expect to be rich and famous; I only wished to live a better life with my husband every day.

I knew better than anybody else that what he said was only because he was angry. But thinking about the future of waiting, I felt hopeless. I called him continuously, contacting him about handling the procedures for divorce as soon as possible.

After a year, we went to the court to handle the divorce procedures. It was a pity that the court could not handle it that afternoon. We were told that we had to go home, wait for their call and then take the judgment. When we left the court, he told me that if it was possible, he would like to begin a new life with me. I agreed with his suggestion and moved out to live with him, though it took me much longer to get to work and back.

That period of life should have been the most happy one we felt after our marriage. We were busy with our work every day, and we planned how we would decorate our new home together. Such days made me feel very relieved. I went out very early every day to go to work, and came back home very late. I had to buy food and cook, have dinner, watch TV and sleep alone. At 2 or 3 o'clock in the morning, the sound of him opening the door used to wake me up. Then I would heat up his supper, and sit on the bed watching him wolf down his meal and repeat that nothing could be more delicious than food cooked at home. At that moment, I felt very gratified and happy.

It was a pity that those days only lasted a very short time. We quarreled again over buying furniture. He again said, "We cannot live together." I knew that he said that just to vent his anger. But I wondered whether divorce was the only way to solve problems. If one quarrel caused one divorce, I would like to keep him company, for I also wanted to see how many times he would divorce because of small quarrels.

When I received the judgment, I asked myself, was it real? It was so easy to turn the dearest couple into two strangers. In less than 20 minutes, we turned from lovers to strangers. Because of an A4 judgment paper, we were no longer lovers. We didn't own the other party any more. We had no relationship any more. The simple and quick procedure of divorce made me shudder. I could hardly believe that fate could be so easily changed, in a moment.

So we turned from unknown to known, from understanding each other to loving each other, from living together to getting married, then from passion to frigidity, from waiting for a divorce to living together until we really divorced. Four years passed, except for being a mother, I felt I had experienced all that a woman could experience in her life. At the time, I had just celebrated my 25th birthday.

After the divorce, he said that he no longer wanted the house, since there was no marriage any more. I didn't belong to him, so there was no need for the house. He said he would feel unhappy living there. But, he said, I could move in. After I did move in, he said he would like to pay a visit. In the big apartment that had almost become our new home, looking at everything so brand-new, he joked, "Since the study is empty, why not let me move in?" I understood him to mean that he was sorry that we had got divorced, and he wanted to come back to live with me. When I heard this, I felt very angry. This was not the period when we loved each other, not the time when he could take all his things away when he was unhappy and lost his temper, and move back little by little afterwards. People often say that a marriage for a woman means the beginning of another life. But for me, even before I had clearly seen my new life and new world, I finished this life in a hurry, and with him in a fit of pique. Thinking about this, I blurted out, "If you have nothing to do with me, you'd better not to come to visit me. Thinking all day about me, how could you begin your new life? In less than two months, how can you change your decision? Everyone should have a sense of responsibility, especially for what one says?" That day, he left very angry, saying that he would never bother me again.

On the same day, soon afterwards, I fell ill. Looking at my watch, it was already 10 p. m. It was impossible to call my parents. Naturally, I thought of him. Whenever I had difficulties, the first person I thought of was him. I took up my mobile phone, and pressed his number, but when I was going to press "send," I stopped, remembering his angry look. I hesitated for half an hour, but at last I nervously and warily pressed the "send" button. The phone rang, and my heart beat faster. When I heard his voice, my tears flowed. I waited for him to reject me, but he didn't. I held the phone for a long time. In fact, in my heart he had never left me. When I was ill, just like before, I expected to nestle up to him and gain his care. In my mind, this divorce was like him leaving one more time after a quarrel before our marriage.... That night, he stayed with me until I had been placed on the last drip bottle, bought a lot of food and took me home. He watched me take medicine, and go to bed, and he finally left at three o'clock in the morning. Several days after that, he would take time out to come to see me no matter how busy he was, helped me to eat something, and left. Before he left, he would continuously exhort me to take care and not catch cold again, and if my illness became serious again, I was to call him no matter what time it was. He said to me: "If you feel unwell, you can call me. My mobile phone will be turned on all the time. "

I wanted to endure all the sufferings and hardship by myself. I hoped that other people would know how strong and independent I was. However, only I understood how hard that was. I had to conquer my emotions. I would prove to him and other people that I was independent, though in my heart I longed for him to give me his hand to hold and a shoulder to cry on.

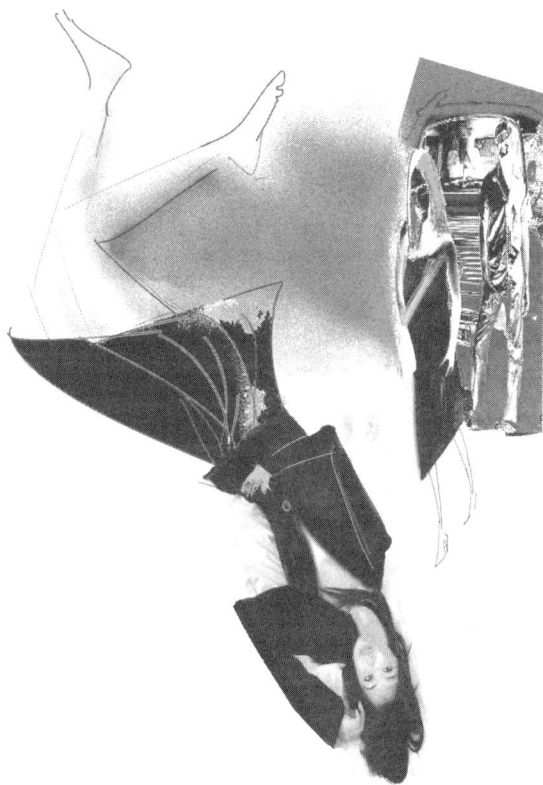

After I recovered from my illness, I didn't call him any more. It was not because I didn't want to call him, but because I wanted to preserve my self-respect. For pitiful dignity that was not worth mentioning, I spent many lonely nights missing him. But when I met him, I said nothing about it, but told him that I lived quite well by myself, free and happy. This situation lasted until the SARS epidemic of 2003. During that time, I often wondered whether divorce was the only way to solve family problems. If the other party was wrong, should I continue the mistakes and not stop them? When he said, "Let's divorce," what did I do? Did I try to save our marriage and solve the problems at that time? I did nothing, I followed him advancing and retreating like a chessman. If he said divorce I would divorce, and if he said no divorce I would not divorce. When he said divorce again, I again echoed what he said. Because of what he said to vent his anger and my irresponsibility, our family of the two disintegrated. Thinking about this, I began to blame myself. Why on earth should we divorce? Because of a lack of love? No, absolutely not! Otherwise, I would not dream of him and think of him endlessly at night, thinking of our past life. Or he would not bring gifts every time he went on business or every time he had a chance, and he would not take me out to dinner to my favorite places. He sighed with feeling how tired his heart was, facing women of all kinds in the outside world, how confused and puzzled he was, and therefore thought of me again and again. He used to tell me: "The women in the outside world have no feelings, no emotions. I think that I will never find the feeling with which we loved each other. Once you have dedicated your feelings and emotions, they are gone, and they will never return. When I see women in the outside world buying the best things greedily with my money, I think of you and the time when we had nothing at all. I know that you lived with me not because I was rich, but because you loved me and treated me well honestly and whole-heartedly." What he said was what I felt in my heart, and so moved me that tears were in my eyes, but I still kept the outwardly strong but inwardly weak attitude, and was not willing to compromise until that day and that short message.

I always believe that the premise for people's getting along is trust. If one party always suspects the other party, then it's impossible for them to get along with each other. This is especially true for couples. Therefore, I never checked his mobile phone or looked into his notebook. But once there was an accidental chance when we went out for dinner. He said he was going to the toilet, and left his seat. Soon his mobile phone rang—it was the sound of a short message. I could hear it. Shall I have a look or not? I asked myself. If it had been in the past, I surely wouldn't have had such an idea. But at that moment, I thought I had changed, it was not that I didn't trust him; it was fear. Every time I met him he would tell me that he had met some woman at another's introduction. I knew how miserable I was in my heart. Though I knew clearly that I was still in his heart, and how much I loved him, because of saving face I never mentioned it. At the same time, I feared so much that one day he would tell me he had finally found a new girlfriend. So thinking, I finally picked up the phone, and furtively read the short message of fewer than 20 words. It had been sent by a woman. This proved two things: one, there was a woman who knew his habits and routine, and two, she cared for him in her own way. I was so afraid that my hands trembled, but I still stored the phone number in my mobile phone, and immediately deleted the message. Because I didn't know the name of the woman, there was no name corresponding to it. Many times I wanted to call that number, and hear that woman's voice, but when I cooled down and thought that I would have nothing to say, and didn't know her name, educational background, life experience, age or appearance, I refrained from calling her. She was just a woman who had a close relationship with him, and it was enough to know this.

Knowing all that, in a constant state of anxiety, I began to try to make him understand in my own way that I still loved him and wished that we could begin our life again as husband and wife. I began to arrange my home. I brought back drawings from places far away when I traveled, and framed them. I displayed shells brought from the seaside in my hometown. I grew flowers and kept fish, hoping to bring back some vitality and make the house like a home. I bought ashtrays from a department store, and put an ashtray in each room in case he came and smoked. I knew that on dark nights when a door was opened, how it would make people feel cold at heart seeing everything in darkness. So I bought a candle and candlestick from a department store, put them on the table of the dining room, and tested them on the day I bought them. I purposely lit the candle before I went out, waited till it was totally dark outside and returned home. Though the candlestick was very small and the candle was not very big, when I opened the door, I felt quite warm in my heart. I felt that the little candle lighted the way to home—my home. I would light the candle every night before I went to sleep. I pretended that he would return any moment. I told myself when he opened the door he would not feel dark and cold, and the little candle's light would make him feel that the home was warm. I remembered one night I had a dream. I dreamed that I was on a bus, and saw an old woman with a little child. The old woman said the child was my husband's, her daughter's husband-to-be. Looking at the child, she said her daughter and my husband were going to get married. I awoke in a panic. Then I cried, and sent him a short message about the dream. I couldn't sleep any more. I sat in the sofa, and watched the candle flame flickering till sunrise. The whole day I was tormented by that terrible dream. It is said that a dream dreamt on a Friday morning will come true, and that dream had been a Friday morning one. I was frightened until the next evening, when I received a phone call from him. He told me that it had been only a dream, and I finally felt reassured. But I couldn't help thinking about it. I thought that it was the time for me to unburden my feelings.

I found a chance one day, when he came to see me. I took him to a supermarket, and asked him to buy Taitai Oral Solution for me. When we lived together, he once bought it for me "as a tonic food to build up my health," because I didn't look well. When I returned home, like before, I asked him to open the bottle. I tasted the liquid, and thought of the past involuntarily. I was immersed in the good memory of the past and was unable to restrain myself. I said to him: "Do you know what I miss most? It is the very short period that we lived together. I felt very happy and satisfied at that time. Do you remember that one day you saw that I didn't drink the Taitai, and then you warmed it for me, and opened the bottle? When I took the bottle from your hand, I felt very gratified. I felt that my work had turned into happiness and satisfaction at the moment when you gave me the bottle. I enjoyed that very much. Since that day, I purposely haven't drunk any, putting the bottle and the thermos on the table, waiting for you to warm the bottle and give it to me. I like the procedure. I like to watch you pour the hot water, test the temperature, open the bottle and give it to me. I enjoy all your actions. I felt like I was the most happy woman in the world at that time, for my husband was expressing endless love and care for me with the most subtle and detailed things. Now people often say that happiness is hard to find, and they don't know what can be called happiness. But I know that in fact a very small thing and an action are enough to make a person feel very happy. For me, when you gave me the bottle, it was a time of happiness. Happiness is not so difficult to find. It is because many times we don't understand it, and neglect it. How about you? Did you feel happy at that time? Do you miss those days?"

"What do you think?" he said. I understood that what he wanted to say was, "Yes, of course!" I said to him: "We should live together again." He rejected me firmly. He said, "It is impossible, because you have ruined everything. You clearly knew that at that time when I was talking about divorce, I was just venting my anger. But you ruined the good days. You are my wound forever." I thought I could understand his resentment, for I had blamed myself for my behavior in the past many times. But I couldn't understand why he said he didn't care for other women at all, and thought I was the best, while he was not willing to begin a new life with me any more. Why? I continued to live alone and keep in contact with him. Of course, the degree of intimacy or indifference was basically determined by him. When we were intimate, we met twice a week. When we were indifferent, it may have been once every two weeks. When we were intimate, he would recall the past with me, and say that I was the best. When we were indifferent, he said that I was a cruel and irresponsible woman, and he would never take me back. Was it because what I had done was not good enough? Or he was testing me? I followed him uncertainly, and I was not sure whether he would like to return to our home. Would he want me to be his wife, caring for him and accompanying him in his future life? My emotions were affected by him, up and down. I tried to pick out good memories of the past from his words. I was once excited for a week because of a sentence of his and was depressed for a week because of a certain expression he used. The ups and downs of my emotions confused me.

For more than a year, I insisted on living in the so-called home, taking care of myself, entertaining by myself, cleaning the big house alone, making it cleaner and cleaner, warmer and warmer. During those days, though I was anxious and nervous, I still chose to wait for him. I also thought of leaving the big house and returning to my parents' home. But I feared that he might return while I was away. I thought as long as I lived there, there were a lamp and a candle for him to lighten his way home. But if I left the house, and locked it, it would not be a home any more. It would be just an empty house no matter how good the furniture and decorations are. I feared that if he returned, he couldn't experience the warmth and romance that a home should have. So I waited in the big and empty house, bitterly waiting to see whether he would return or not.

## On the occasion of the Spring Festival, I gradually understood that waiting like this was futile.

I remembered that you once said what you worried about most was how I spent the Spring Festival. That Spring Festival was very important for me. It was after that Spring Festival that I gradually realized that if I waited like that nothing would come of it.

After you had written the story on my intention to resume my marriage, I felt a little bit assured. At that time, I thought that, anyway, I had spoken out my ideas, and you couldn't continue to drag me along. Therefore, after that, when I met him I told him that there was a newspaper in which there were many things that I wanted to say to him, and I hoped that he could read it. At that time he might feel somewhat surprised. He said that he would not like to read it right then, as he had no time, and he told me to send it to his office. I did so. At that time I thought that no matter what he would say, I must do it, for if neither of us spoke out our ideas clearly, we would misunderstand each other forever.

At that time our relationship was a bit strange. I could feel that in fact he also felt it was somewhat a pity. After all, our marriage had lasted only a short time. We broke up when we were angry. But now we understand that we should view an issue from different aspects. At that time we didn't understand that, we just got angry and had to vent our anger without considering the consequences. He still came to see me, and he occasionally cared for my life. So I had a feeling or illusion that this was a hint that he wanted to save the family. I thought I was conservative, at least about marriage. At that time I still had the intention of attaining a satisfactory result; I never thought of loving someone else, and acquaintances assured me that it was a good thing for two people who had broken up in a fit of pique to be reconciled. Because after all that unhappiness, the two would realize the importance of treasuring love and getting along well with each other. To tell the truth, at that time I agreed with that. Sometimes when I thought of falling in love with someone else, developing an emotional relationship with a stranger, I felt inexplicably uncomfortable. Maybe because of fear of the unknown, I was rather weak emotionally, and couldn't look back on our marriage objectively. I believe now that if two people really treasure their family and the feelings in their hearts, they will not divorce no matter what happens. If they divorce easily, there must be other problems involved. Or if the feeling really ends and they live together again, they will see a big gap every day. Can they feel happy from the bottom of their hearts? If they continue to quarrel with each other, it will be too late for them to repent. Therefore, from this point of view, compared with falling love with someone else and resumption of marriage, it may be more possible for the latter to hurt people. The reason is quite simple: The two know where the wounds of the other party are. The next hurt will be in the old place, and the hurt will only be deeper.

It is pity that at that time I didn't understand these things. Before that Spring Festival, I didn't hear any news of him. The newspaper had been sent to him, and I believed that he had read it, but he said nothing. I sounded him on whether he had read it. He said he had read it. I tried to continue to talk about it, but he changed the subject. Maybe I began to give up then.

The Spring Festival was coming. Although I had not as much expectation as before, I still felt that the Spring Festival was the day for reunion. Anyhow, we were husband and wife, and we had not begun to fall in love with other people. I would prepare a meal for him, and let him return home to eat. I felt sad about the fact that the home that was built by the efforts of the two of us had been lost very quickly.

On the morning of the first day of the Spring Festival, I got up quite early to tidy up the house. He had promised to come and have supper with me. There was only some memory of him left in my heart. But at that time, I still thought that I should make him feel that the home was warm, my heart never left the home, and if he was willing to come back, we could begin our life again. Encouraged by these ideas, I felt quite happy as I was doing the housework.

However, while I was wiping the floor, a piece of tile dropped on my hand and cut it. I went to a hospital about one bus stop away. A doctor treated the wound, and put a stitch in it. He said there was no anesthetic, so I was in great pain. My hand and half my arm were bandaged.

Though our marriage had been short, it was I who took care of him. It was almost impossible for me to gain care from him. What do women want? They really don't want money from men, nor want to be served by men, nor want a big house and a nice car. I think what I want is quite simple. I only want one thing. Maybe someone would look down upon me, thinking that I am not practical. Maybe others would think I am easily fooled. It doesn't matter. What I value most is my mood. If I am in a good mood, I like to do anything.

He came to see me that day, as arranged. I told him what had happened, and apologized for not being able to cook for him. He immediately became unhappy. He said if he had known, he would not have come. Since he couldn't have the meal, it was better for him to go back. He asked me to go back to my parents' home as soon as possible so that my mother could take care of me. Of course, he didn't forget to ask me if I had enough money. Do you know what I felt at that time? I felt like I was a burden, and I was a person who didn't keep promises and got others into trouble. I knew that he had money, and didn't mind giving me money. We divorced not because of these things. But when he showed that he cared for me by way of giving me money, I really felt uncomfortable.

After he went away that day, I knew that if I waited continuously, there would still be no result. I remembered my life after the divorce. It had been really hard. I was the only person in such a big house. I didn't know what to do. I looked here and there, standing and walking in the house. I would spend the whole night like this. I listened for the sound of steps in the corridor. Sometimes when the sound of steps came nearer and nearer, I felt nervous without any reason, thinking that the sound of the person was related to me, and maybe he had returned. When the sound died away I was very disappointed. Then the process began again, till I was tired and fell asleep.

Such a life is like resigning oneself to death. I put all my hope on someone else, but if that person didn't respond, you would have nothing. What about yourself?

After that day I didn't contact him again. I thought that, as my marriage had ended, I must find myself. Whether I could be happy in the future depended on myself, waiting for somebody else was no use.

**Sometimes the image of a person is totally ruined by a very small detail. But something we consider important is hard to be compromised in the end.**

If you don't mention that I had a blind date, I will not mention it. Sometimes I think having a blind date is interesting. Two persons who don't know each other are described by the marriage broker. Some descriptions are true and trustworthy, but some may be false. Could the views represent anyone? The two, after hearing the introduction and feeling that the conditions of the other party are rather good, decide to meet. The marriage broker will not follow them after they meet, the development of the relationship between the two relies on the two themselves. How many accidental factors are in this? I can't say clearly.

It is not easy for me to accept having a blind date. I am not a critical person. You may feel that in daily life I am an easygoing person. But I believe that no one can be easygoing when meeting a stranger for the first time, unless the person himself is very casual. Being easygoing and casual are two totally different concepts. The man who took my hand and disgusted you was introduced by one of my relatives. In fact he is not a bad man. The situation at that time was related to my state of mind.

The man was a little older than I. He had never been married, and was in the insurance business. The job sounds a bit uninteresting, right? I also thought so. But at that time people who knew him insisted that he had a stable income and had a good family background. At that time I also thought that it didn't matter, as I had made up my mind to fall in love with a new man. To have a blind date was not a shame, so I decided to meet him.

Maybe because I have worked for a long time in foreign companies, no matter what I have in my mind, I still make sure that I dress properly. I prepared my clothes, and dressed up carefully. I thought that we should respect each other, for it was the first time for us to meet. He had on a bright shirt decorated with elephant patterns. He said he had bought it in Thailand. Then we had a meal together. After the meal, he suggested we go singing karaoke together. I had no reason to refuse, so I followed him.

His singing left me with a bad impression. I thought that it was rather laughable. I even forget what song he was singing. He sang it with deep emotion, and was very concentrated. In the song there was a sentence which I didn't hear clearly, I only clearly heard him sing loudly the words "kuaizishou." I felt puzzled at that time. It seemed that the pronunciation should be "guizishou (executioner)." I thought that it might be my problem. I listened carefully, waiting to see if the words would appear in the next section. As I expected, it finally came, still the passionate "kuaizishou." I didn't laugh at that time, I really could not laugh. Did anyone have words unknown? Were there times for anyone to pronounce and write wrong words? It was not something serious, but I suddenly felt very sad, for an unknown reason. I thought that I just did not want to spend my life with a man who engaged in insurance and sang "kuaizishou." You can say I am too critical, but I just have no desire to contact him again.

He insisted on walking me home, and on the way he held my hand, in spite of my protests. When I got home it took me a long time to do one thing— wash my hands. In the past, when I saw girls in films who cried and washed their hands, I thought they were affected. But that day I really experienced that feeling. It was just as if my hands could never be washed clean. Did I think that the man was really dirty? Maybe not. I just felt so terrible. When I finally stopped washing my hands, I sat on the sofa and cried aloud. There was only myself at home, so I cried as I liked. There are so many people in such a big world, but it is so difficult to find one that you can accept from the bottom of your heart. But I really didn't want to compromise.

People often urged me to find a man with good salary while I was still young, with a good job and good looks, then get married as soon as possible, bear a child, and live a stable life, and not to be too stubborn about some "useless things." I understood what they meant. What can be called useless things? It refers to spiritual requirements, such as details like "kuaizishou." I am telling you this, for you know me, and you can understand me. If I speak to other people, I am afraid that they will criticize me for being "too critical." But I really feel that I should at least find someone who can communicate with me, with a kind character and interested in culture. Now I have a stronger and stronger feeling that when we look for a partner, there are some things we shouldn't neglect. Whether the two are suitable or not in the end can be clearly discovered when they retire. When they are young, they are busy with their jobs and housework. They go to work five days a week, and when they go back home they are tired. If they have a child, they will be even more tired. At last, when they are retired they face each other every day, and suddenly find out that the other party never really understood his or her spouse, and they have nothing to talk about after all. I think that this can be basically viewed as a tragic marriage. Therefore, I believe that if one person has a stable profession and the ability to make a living, he or she can be regarded as possessing the basic material conditions. I believe in mutual efforts. The indispensable factor is the cultural quality of the man. Without it, even if the material conditions are very good I will not accept the man.

Because of these stubborn ideas, I missed "an excellent man," my relative said, but I don't think so.

It was in the summer of 2005, when the same relative introduced another man to me. He had graduated from a famous university, and had a stable job with a salary of over 10,000 yuan. He had a house and a car, and was several years older than I. My relative specially noted that "he often goes abroad on business" and "his parents are intellectuals."

At that time I had become especially calm, and did not reject the concept of blind dating. But to tell the truth, I didn't have much expectation. In the matter of love, you cannot draw a conclusion after the first meeting.

One night, my relative called me at about ten o'clock, and asked me to go to a bar, saying that the man was waiting for me. I didn't hate bars, and didn't think that there was anything wrong about night life, but I didn't feel like going. My relative was not very old, and said I was too conservative, for ten o'clock was not too late. I was adamant, and so the date was postponed until the next day.

On my way to the date, I thought that such a well educated man with a major in a foreign language should be very talkative. I thought about what topics we could talk about. Was he interested in films? I had just seen a French film called *Butterfly*; I might talk about that. If we talked about Chinese films, it didn't matter. At that time, people were all arguing about *Hands in the Hair*. I reviewed the films I had seen and the books I had read. I even thought that maybe the man would consider me a shallow person. It was a pity that in the end my worries were groundless. In fact, I couldn't understand fully what he and his friends talked about.

When we sat down to dine, he ordered a big bottle of strong liquor. He didn't care that he had driven his car there, and had to drive back. After drinking for a while, he and his friends became talkative. They said that the previous night, when I hadn't "done them a favor," they had played all night the "Game of Killing." I didn't know what that game was. Later, they asked me what kinds of entertainment I enjoyed in my spare time. I said I liked watching movies and also reading. "There are so many DVDs of films nowadays, many of them quite classic." At last, I could not speak any longer. I felt that I was a weird person. They all said to me: "We never watch movies, for they are not interesting or funny at all." They asked me where I went in the evening. I said I seldom went out in the evening. They said, "Do you like climbing mountains and going to parks?" I felt I was really "old fashioned." At the same time, I thought they were old fashioned. I even suspect that their lifestyle was not a healthy one. At this time, one suddenly suggested adding Coca-Cola to the liquor, saying that it would then taste like XO brandy. They suddenly became very excited, and drank excessively. I asked myself: Is he the man who was said to be gentle and cultivated?

The man offered to drive me home, but I refused because he had drunk too much.

At last I went home by myself. My entire dream about culture and communication had evaporated. I felt that I could not marry a drunkard.

He sent me many e-mails after that, offering to develop our relationship. But I refused. I told him we were not suited to each other. My relative got angry, saying that he would never help me again. "Where could you find a man with such good conditions?" I thought for a while, and said that I really didn't agree. Not mentioning other things, just by driving after drinking he showed that he didn't even treasure himself, so how could other people rely on him?

I am still single. Now that I recall those two persons, I realize that they were not bad men, and surely there will be good girls who want to live with them. But I don't.

## Interviewer's Notes

### Stupid Women Save Their Marriage, and Strong Women Save Themselves

At the end of September 2008, the Beijing TV Society channel was to make a program about me and my work. The producer wished to let one of my interviewees talk about "What did An Dun mean to the interviewees?" My first reaction was rejection. As a reporter, I can understand the purpose of it, but as a social worker who has been engaged in individual experience investigation for a long time, I thought it was a very "dangerous" attempt, as I didn't want to let the calm life of an interviewee of mine be disturbed unnecessarily just to explain the value of my work. After all, many of my interviewees confide their private thoughts to me alone.

As I was hesitating, Yi Ming suddenly came to visit me. She had been traveling alone in Austria, the Czech Republic and Hungary. She brought a doll for my daughter. She wanted to ask me why so many people would "fall in love in Prague," while why didn't she. After a while, I told her of the TV offer.

Yi Ming was keen to be interviewed by the TV people. I warned her that her private thoughts could be broadcast for all of Beijing to learn about.

Yi Ming laughed, and said, "I don't care. I haven't been a grumbling maid for many years."

What she said was true, and I am very lucky to "witness" the changes in her from 2003 till now, seeing her change from a so-called "grumbling maid" to a healthy, sunny, independent and capable strong woman. Sometimes I even worry that if she revels in her happy life, will she make most men who are eager to find a woman lovely and pliable like a little bird hang back?

Even before the interview in 2003, Yi Ming and I were already old acquaintances. We used to meet on the same Internet forum, leaving messages for each other, and she occasionally would tell me something about her moods or recent situation. At that time, we never thought of meeting formally. I knew that Yi Ming had been divorced for almost a year. But she never left her original home, which was still as it was when her former husband left (She was still accustomed to calling him "my husband"). The house was very big, and for one person it seemed very spacious. When she was alone at home, she was too lazy to cook meals. She walked here and there in the rooms. When she walked in the house she couldn't help feeling sad, for nothing was the same as before.

Later I wrote on Internet to her the sentence from *Knife Man*: "I think I shouldn't go away. Maybe if I wait for you for a moment you will return." When I wrote these words to her, I felt quite sad, and indistinctly felt that it was unfair for her. Why should she wait? Why should it always be women who are waiting? Even if she had a deep love for him, was it worth wasting her youth? Of course, when she was angry, she would say, "Who does he think he is?"

Later, I began to encourage her to speak out. Why not tell him what you are waiting for? Why not let him know your wish? Why not let him answer "Yes" or "No", "Love" or "No Love"? Why should you live like this, suffering in silence for the rest of your life?

After our first meeting, we continued to write to each other. I told her that I would wait, just like her waiting for her man to return. I would wait until the day she was ready to let me express her feelings in my newspaper columns. Of course, maybe that day would never come.

When I went to Yi Ming's home that year, my first feeling was very uncomfortable. I didn't tell her that my eyes almost gushed with tears when she cooked a hamburger for me. I saw too many traces by her former husband. Their wedding photos faced the door, as if welcoming guests. I thought of the room Zhou Puyuan had left for Shi Ping in *Thunderstorm*. This divorced woman had never left her marriage. If such a woman couldn't wait for what she wanted, what about her future?

The interview ended at dusk. Yi Ming saw me off to the gate of the apartment compound. I didn't know why, but looking at her standing in front of me I felt that she was trembling.

A few days later, I received a letter from her. It read:

An Dun,

I always think that I am a materialist, but when one is at one's wits' end, it seems it is very natural that one hopes to find some comforts. I found a fortune teller, and asked her to explain the ups and downs in my marriage, and to explain the reasons for the situation. She was willing to help me, but such help was not free. She demanded 3,000 yuan. She reminded me: "You don't have much time. If you don't grasp the opportunity, you will lose it, and you will regret it for the rest of your life." She said I only had 40 days to get him to return to me. I felt as if the next day were the day for an examination which I hadn't prepared for. I wanted to recite something but I couldn't. It seemed that I was destined to fail. I wanted to take care of him, and I wanted to tell him how much I loved him and how much I regretted our divorce. But I didn't know how to say it, or how to do it. I even wished it were windy or snowy every day so that I could have valid reasons to care for him. But what could I do? It was impossible for me to ask him every day what he was busy doing, if he had proper meals and sleep. After all, we had no such relationship any more. I was afraid that my excessive enthusiasm would so scare him that he wouldn't dare to answer my calls. So many nights I wanted to call him but didn't dare to do so. Every time when I finally found an excuse to call him, I would prepare how to speak to him, thinking of all his possible answers. Every time when I called him, when the phone was connected, my heart began to beat fast. How nervous I was! My heart beat fast at every opportunity of calling him!

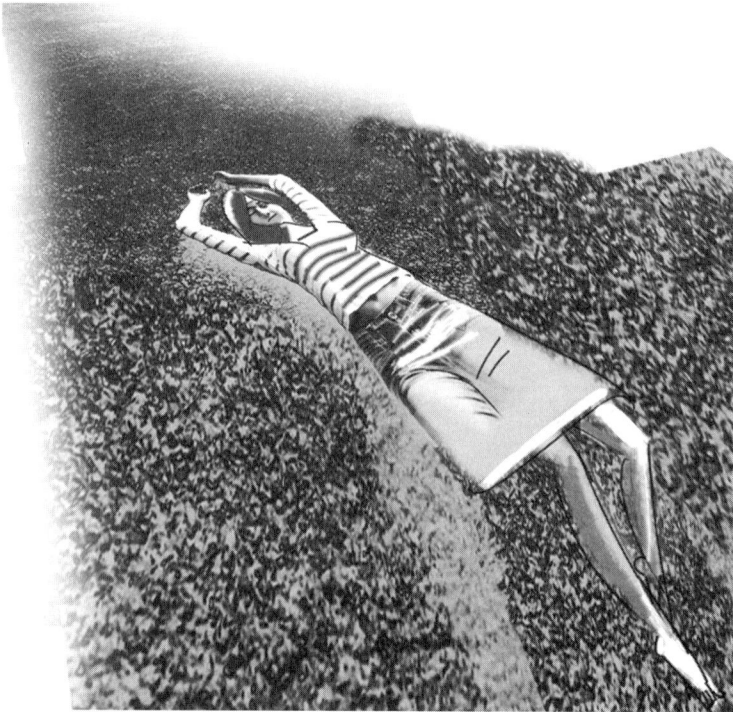

That day, when you came to my home, I didn't have enough time to show you the whole apartment. There is a wall that I leave empty. I am waiting, waiting for the time of our reconciliation. Then I will use the wall and call it a happy wall, putting pictures of us at different ages on the wall in different frames. At first there will be two persons, and after that there will be three persons. Every visitor to our home will see our life, happiness and how our family has grown from that wall. Can you understand? Every time I think about it, I always feel very happy about this idea, which is not so creative. When I have nothing to do, I will think of a name for our child, and how to raise him in the future. I would take pictures if I were pregnant. When he was born, I would take pictures of him when he celebrated his birthday every year. When he grew up and got married, I would compile the pictures into a collection, and give it to our lovely child as a gift. The collection would be like my happy wall, on which there was the growing process of the crystal of our love. The painstaking efforts would be because of our deep love for each other. I never tell him this, and I am not sure if he would also feel happy from the bottom of his heart at all my ideas for our home and future.

But where is my future?

Yi Ming

Many times I often hesitate in the process of interviews. I often think that I am not a person who is good at comforting other people, and for many people, comforts seem very cheap and useless. So, when I wrote back to Yi Ming, I didn't use warm words, but wrote with enough kindness and reason, as follows:

Yi Ming,

Your letter today made me think about many things at the same time. I'm a bit confused.

I have also seen the film *Unfaithful* that you mentioned. At that time what I thought most was, what is love? In fact, a large part of love is tolerance. Sometimes it is also connivance. It is true. From my point of view, the highest state of one's love for another is to respect and appreciate every choice of the other person. It's also the self-discipline caused by the thanks for the respect and appreciation from the one who loves me. It sounds a bit tongue-twisting, right? But I think I have made it clear. This is also my ideal.

We have talked so long that maybe you have not realized that when you talked about your former husband, you were always exultant and a bit shy. I think that in fact your situation is rather difficult. Your heart follows every tiny change in him. You always want to find evidence that it is beneficial to you to desire a "resumption of marriage" in clues of his words and actions. This is also the reason for you to insist on waiting continuously. I can understand you. But, as an outsider, I also want to tell you that when you have too strong a desire it will cause you to make wrong judgments, and will mislead you. I think you should understand my meaning. And I insist on believing that a man shouldn't hesitate—even more, he shouldn't try to evade a question by changing the subject when the woman has clearly told him her wishes. He should give a definite answer to her, so that neither will waste time, and so that the woman will not be unable to extricate herself from her plight. If it is possible, I hope, that you can deliver my words to your former husband. I don't care about his view of me. I think that should be the right way, and more fair to you.

You are right that we should have a sense of responsibility. But I want to add that we should not only be responsible for the past, but should also be responsible for the future. We should be responsible for other people, but that does not mean abandoning responsibility for ourselves. If you get your wish fulfilled, you can regard your efforts as well recompensed. If you finally have to abandon each other, then please believe me that in your future life you will find your beloved; it's just that you can't see him at present.

You think that I am obdurate or cruel? I don't think so. Reason seems a little cold, but what people need most is still reason.

An Dun

On January 16, 2003, Yi Ming left a message for me on my mobile phone. She told me that she had made up her mind that she wanted me to put her story in the paper.

Then I abandoned the draft I had prepared before, and I took out and rearranged the record of our talks and all our e-mails. After two days it would be the Spring Festival. I couldn't imagine how this woman who was waiting for love would spend the festival.

Later the Oral Factual Record of the interview with Yi Ming was published on my page in the *Beijing Youth Daily*. The title of it was "I Would Like to Believe that God Blesses Faithful People." In summary, Yi Ming is a lonely woman who has made every effort to save her marriage. She wants to use the long memory to wake up her man, who has left home, letting him see that she is still standing in the old place and waiting for him to return home.

I remember that when the newspapers were sold that morning, we pasted the article on the Internet. She and I paid attention to the reaction of readers together. At that time it seemed that we had some divergence. I insisted on believing that more people would support me, and would think it was irresponsible for her to waste her youth like this. I knew that Yi Ming's former husband never told her whether he would like to marry her again or not, but he didn't refuse her absolutely. Except for not answering the question, he treated Yi Ming as well as before. His kindness sometimes made her gradually sink into loneliness and helplessness. Because she didn't know what his ideas were, she dared not be indiscreet. Because she could always feel some hope from his silence, she encouraged herself to persist all the time, being afraid that all her previous efforts would be wasted. Because she feared that if she urged him, he would feel uncomfortable, she had to suppress her feelings. At last, she still didn't know what he wanted to do, but she thought she would grow old helplessly. I told her this, but she didn't argue with me, just saying, as always: "I will wait and see." Waiting for what? She just waited to deliver a newspaper to her former husband, because in it I had written very clearly that he must give the woman who has been waiting for him a definite answer. I thought, "Do you think that you are somebody? How can you let such a woman wait for you in an empty house, consigning her to death?"

At that time, on our forum there were many net friends who were paying attention to Yi Ming and her problems. They all said that if she wanted to begin a new life she must give herself a deadline, such as after the Spring Festival she would not wait for him anymore. Not long after that it was the Spring Festival. What I worried about most was not that Yi Ming could not get a definite answer, but that if she spent the Spring Festival alone she would feel much lonelier than ever. And I worried about her mood.

I did not expect that the accidental wounding of Yi Ming would be a turn for the better—she gradually began to realize that her life needed a change.

As more people joined our website group Yi Ming turned from being a net friend who enlightened others when she had time to being the website administrator. Many new girls called her "sister." Some net friends talked with me in private and asked me about the present situation of Yi Ming, and some warmhearted friends even tried to introduce boyfriends to her. Maybe I still have some selfish motives, but I always worry that after readers read her story about her desire for resumption of marriage they might still think that Yi Ming is still yearning for her old marriage and will lose the chance to be pursued by more excellent men.

From the summer of 2004, Yi Ming worked with us to set up the website. One of her good friends also became my friend. Lao Zhang, who was in America, used to help us with our website. Late one night, Lao Zhang called me, and said, "There's something we must talk about." The topic was Yi Ming and her last blind date. Lao Zhang was furious at the man for taking liberties with Yi Ming. Immediately afterwards, I called Yi Ming and asked her why she hadn't told me about that blind date. She told me that it had been because she didn't like the idea of blind dates, but had no choice. We talked casually, and strayed from the subject. After I hung up the receiver, the more I thought about it the more uncomfortable I felt in my mind. On that day I felt that life was really very unfair: Every day I face people who fall in love, some happily and some unhappily. Why is there no love in Yi Ming's life?

The following evening I posted a new topic with the title "Seeking Marriage for My Sister" on our forum. I briefly introduced Yi Ming, and left my contact numbers. Of course, I decided by myself some specific conditions a man should meet to be considered suitable. Yi Ming continued "blind dating," but every time was a failure. Meanwhile, she changed her job to go to work at another foreign company which paid her a higher salary. But she became even busier, and seemed to abandon her quest for love.

Yi Ming has her own blog on our website, and I am one of her most faithful readers. From her words I can understand her mood, especially what she can't say to me when she talks with me face to face. Through reading her diary, I can feel that Yi Ming has become stronger and more optimistic little by little. I firmly believe that she will meet a man, and they will be fated to really love each other.

Yi Ming wrote a short essay on her birthday, titled "A Gift to Myself." I know that it was not written for me, but I would still like to use her own words as the end of my interview notes.

Compared with my first interview by An Dun and its publication in her newspaper, this time I felt quite natural, less nervous and uneasy and with more confidence and calmness. If the last time I tried to recall a person who didn't belong to me, this time I wanted to tell all my family members and friends who care for me, including myself, that there will always be sunshine and hope tomorrow. When the interview was published in the newspaper, it was my birthday. I think maybe it was the best birthday gift, and one I had sent myself.

It seems that the dream of all children is to grow up as soon as possible. When they grow up they can do anything they like, they will not be restricted by their parents, they will not have to do their homework and sacrifice the TV programs they like and go to bed early. When I was a little child, I didn't have a very definite reason for growing up, but just blindly wanted to grow up as soon as possible. But I never thought the price for growing up was that my parents would become old. I always remember that when I was a little girl, one evening, when I was going to bed, Mum was tidying up the room and told me she was going to throw away the garbage. I told her that I was afraid to be alone in bed. She comforted me, saying, "Within only two minutes after you close your eyes, and then when you open your eyes, I'll be back." So I closed my eyes. Time passed quickly, I have grown up, and am an adult now.

Though I have grown up, my parents are still worrying about me. They are not happy letting me live alone, worrying that if I fell sick there would be no one to take care of me. They also worry that I might feel lonely. So Mum asked me to call her every night.

I can understand Mum's worry, but every time I tell her not to worry about me, but to be assured that there will always a good man waiting for me. What do I want? I think it's just the kind of so-called ordinary people's life—having breakfast together, going to work, coming back home from the office, cooking supper, watching TV, and chatting, day after day. I will add that in fact there is still one important point, that is, I hope when I am not at home my husband won't even be able to find his socks. Every one has vanity, and this can be regarded as my vanity. I think that if I insist upon my ideas and believe in love, such a man will in the end enter my life.

On birthdays I always make a wish. My wish is that Dad and Mum can stay healthy. I hope that from this day on, I will begin my new life, for no matter what happens, there is always hope in the future!

Recalling all that I know about Yi Ming, especially when I heard about her travels and see new souvenirs in her bookcases and pictures in her photo albums, I always sighed with emotion. Maybe ordinary girls like her are like this; at first, their dream in life for happiness is always connected with love and a man. Like in fairytales, at last, a prince riding a white horse—Prince Charming—will surely appear, "and they will live happily ever after." Girls who have such a good fate are surely very lucky and worth blessing. But not all girls will have such smooth lives, like Yi Ming and thousands upon thousands of women like her. Even when they have made all their emotional efforts, they still cannot keep their first love. They are destined to lose their love, heal themselves, learn to stand on their own feet and face the future with a healthy mind. Some people are successful, and they regain their love and marriage. Others may have a long way to go, with expectations in their hearts, and make a living independently. I think Yi Ming is one of the latter. But when she becomes more independent economically and spiritually, her expectations for a man to bring happiness for her will fade, and she will yearn more to create a satisfactory life by herself. Prince Charming may come tomorrow, or he may never come. So what should women do? Yi Ming is a very good example of the saying "Stupid women save their marriage, and strong women save themselves."

# "Unemployment", the Peak of "My Career"

**Time of interview**: April 20, 2008

**Place**: Beijing Kerry Center

Wang Tao, male, 37, comes from Shijiazhuang City, Hebei Province. He once served in the 63rd Corps of the People's Liberation Army. Later, he was admitted to the Military Economics Academy of the People's Liberation Army. He engaged in management work at Shijiazhuang Bethune International Peace Hospital after graduation. Wang settled down in Beijing after he was transferred to civilian work. He is now working at the Center for Environmental Health of Xicheng District, Beijing. Wang volunteers to curb and discourage uncivilized behavior like spitting and littering during his spare time. His service time so far has added up to 1,000 hours, with success recorded in over 20,000 cases since 2006. He set up the Beijing Green Woodpecker Environmental Protection Organization and China Anti-spitting Network. He has been honored as one of the "Good People in Beijing," "Moral Model in Beijing" and "Sino-British Non-governmental Green Messenger" since 2007 for his impressive volunteer service.

## What on earth had happened to China's public image?

My sensitivity to environmental health can probably be attributed to my work experience. I like traveling, and tried to learn English by myself a long time ago. During the learning process, I found that in some public places in foreign countries, cities open to Chinese tourists in particular, signs saying no spitting in Chinese can be seen in public places. I mean, in foreign countries with different language environments, there are even tips specially for Chinese. Isn't that enough to make us ask what on earth has happened to China's public image?

Some of my friends come from foreign countries, and they have asked me why Chinese people like to spit in the street, and didn't you think it was a kind of private excretion? I was struck dumb by the question, yet for face saving, I could only tell them that according to the traditional Chinese medicine, spitting out phlegm itself is supposed to be good for the health, and the only problem is that some people paid little attention to where they spit. But it is a lame excuse. After all, this has definitely been one of our bad habits for many years. Now our country and cities are becoming more and more beautiful, and China will soon host the Olympic Games. These phlegm marks and discarded rubbish are extremely disgusting. Almost every person has started to pay attention to his/ her clothes and appearance as incomes rise. Yet some people don't seem to be able to protect our environment while paying attention to their personal hygiene. I'm afraid that it's not simply a bad habit; they lack a sense of social responsibility.

Am I a person with a sense of social responsibility? I feel that I am. I'm not a native of Beijing, but my family and I live here now. I do hope the whole environment outside my small family can truly become a clean, beautiful and modern international metropolis. Besides, I also hope the whole country, not just Beijing, will be clean and beautiful. We Chinese would be proud of that. I think what I say makes sense. I don't want my own apartment to be criticized as messy, and I don't want people to think I live a rather poor life. Similarly, I don't want foreigners to feel that both China and the Chinese are dirty. That was probably what inspired me to do city cleaning volunteer work.

Though not a fan of sports, I still feel extremely happy about Beijing's successful bid for the Olympics, as I think this is an opportunity to improve the sense of social responsibility of all Chinese, as well as an opportunity to present and promote China to the rest of the world. Just like you have to clean up your apartment to welcome guests, we should clean up Beijing when foreigners are gathering in Beijing for the Olympic Games.

I was thinking about this when watching Beijing's successful bid for the Olympics on TV. I felt that there would be lots of meaningful things to do, yet could not just bring them to mind. The issue of "anti-spitting" has haunted me for more than half a year. Then I happened to watch a TV program called "Action Now", produced by Beijing TV station. The program was themed "Looking for Spitters". Volunteers would give the spitter a piece of tissue paper to wipe off the phlegm. This program was very interesting, as spitters were extremely embarrassed when they were caught. I was just thinking at that time, it would be better to behave properly earlier rather than be embarrassed now. You know, I work in an environmental health department, and I know exactly that spitting mark removal is really an annoying problem for environmental health staff. Ordinary cleaning doesn't work, and the dirt can only be flushed away with a great deal of water, and Beijing is short of water. It is also unrealistic to wipe off the marks one by one by cleaning staff with cloth and paper. What should we do? Actually, we have to address the problem from its source. Specifically, to enhance people's awareness. Everyone shall be aware of the fact that spitting is bad, uncivilized and unhealthy. Any decent and self-respecting person should not spit in public. To put it simply, spitting is actually related to every person. So long as everyone can stop spitting, then there will be no marks left. That was what I thought when watching that program. I felt that someone should take care of this issue, I mean, to curb and correct this uncivilized behavior at all times, and to remind those people without a sense of environmental protection about civilized behavior.

I was wondering what I should do if I was asked to take care of this issue on that day.

What the environmental health staff do was far from a decent job in the eyes of many people in the past. And they have been looked down upon for a long time. As a result, if a cleaning worker tried to discourage people from spitting, he/she would be snapped at or something like that. Some workers, however, are still brave enough to remonstrate with people who litter and spit. Yet most workers prefer to clear the dirt rather than stop spitters to avoid disputes, you know, which may affect their normal work. Besides, spitting is actually an issue involving the quality of the citizen, city management, and the management committee of the municipal people's government and disease control center of the health organs, among others.

As a citizen of Beijing, I think I have a responsibility to do something for the environment. I am also a clean and decent person. If I tried to stop a spitter, would he dare to look down on me? Am I more powerful? Actually, I think this is the case. When I really started to do this, many things occurred later that finally proved that what I thought was right. To this end, when we are offering initial training for new volunteers, we always stress that, as a volunteer, you should first have a clean image. You are a volunteer, but also a living example.

So when you see the volunteers from Green Woodpecker offer services in the street, even when they crouch down to remove sputum and pick up rubbish, you know that although all these things are dirty, yet they are clean themselves.

**I hoped that one day I could motivate the people of all cities nationwide to stop spitting.**

I always asked myself some questions, like what would I do if I were snapped at or humiliated? What would I do to the sputum on the ground if spitters did not follow what you suggested? The last question was most frequently asked. In fact, I was asking myself if I could crouch down to remove others' sputum with tissue paper in public places before so many people. Can I do that? Can I do that without any regret? I know it was easier said than done, as what I have to do was really a challenge psychologically, and also the greatest difficulty for us volunteers.

Before going into the street, I practiced at home behind my wife's back. "Did you just spit? This is unhealthy. Here is some tissue paper. Could you please wipe it up? " I said to the mirror. I also practiced to wiping stuff up myself.

This process really took a long time. I bought myself a laptop and a video camera. I felt that I should record what I was going to do, and this was the starting point of my exploration into the meaning of life. I also bought necessary equipment like tissue paper, gloves and clips at that time. I kept all these things secretly in a large plastic bag in a small corner of my apartment. They are still there. I also made myself a small badge with my name and the words "City Cleaning Volunteer" on it.

I finally began on May 4, 2006, Youth Day, in Tian'anmen Square. I wanted to start the campaign from Tian'anmen Square, as it is the heart of our motherland. I also hoped that one day what I did could motivate all cities nationwide to stop spitting while carrying forward the energetic spirit of "May 4"!

As a former soldier, I felt I was about to fight on that day, and prepared myself psychologically. I wore a suit and freshened myself up carefully, as I wanted my image to be more convincing. I brought the video camera to record the experience. And I also brought over 20 packets of tissue paper. I was thinking that if any spitter followed what I advised and wiped up his or her sputum, I would give him or her one packet of tissues as a reward. I set off at dawn. I lied to my wife, saying that I had to work overtime due to some emergency at the company.

I arrived at Tian'anmen Square at the crack of dawn, when people had just finished watching the flag-raising ceremony. The first person I came across was a thin middle-aged man, not very tall. He was at the northern edge of the square. I said, "Excuse me, please wait a second! You have just spat, and...." But he just disappeared into the crowd. I then wiped up his mess. Before I did so, I paused and said to myself: "Yes, you can do it!" With such encouragement, I concentrated my attention and took the dirt away to the dustbin nearby. I didn't care too much if it was dirty or not, actually I was very happy and moved greatly. I know that I can do whatever I want as I have already broken the barriers in my heart.

I removed the sputum by myself. Though the process was difficult, yet what I had to do is just to convince myself. And it would be more difficult to advise people to wipe it up, which requires sound communication, great courage, a nice tone and a friendly expression. You should also be well

prepared to be scolded.

    The second spitter I met was a peddler selling postcards in the square. I went to him immediately and said what I had practiced at home. He looked at me and asked, "What do you do?" I replied that I was a volunteer. He then asked who sent me there, and I replied I sent myself there. He looked at me as if I were a monster. I passed him the tissue paper, and said, "Could you please wipe it up? It's not good behavior. If you don't remove it, I will do it for you. " The peddler was very angry. Many businesspeople around kicked up a fuss and said, "You wipe it up. Don't let another person do it for you. " Though reluctant, he finally removed it. I gave him a packet of tissue paper, and said, "Thank you. Please take some tissue paper with you, and spit into it. It will do no harm to the environment. " He took the tissue, and left. I knew that I had been successful, and the barrier to communication had also been cracked.

    I went back home at dusk that day. The first thing I did was to hide all my tools as soon as possible. Then I started to write down what had happened. That day was unforgettable. It was a brand-new start. I also felt very powerful.

## "China would be a better place if everyone behaved like you."

I thought I should make this campaign bigger by attracting more volunteers after that first experience. If I were a woodpecker, I could do very little on my own, no matter how hard I tried. But if there were such woodpeckers around every corner in Beijing, how great our power would be! What I thought inspired me to launch an anti-spitting activity. I motivated over 60 relatives and friends on QQ to take part in the activity. We agreed to gather at Times Square, Xidan, on July 1, 2006 to fight against spitting. Only six people attended that day. They later became the founding members of the Green Woodpecker movement. I came to know that I had friends with the same ambition, and I was not alone.

Setbacks can occur in anything you do. The one thing I felt most frustrated about during my two years as a volunteer was an incident in Tuanjiehu Park. Several bare-chested men were smoking in the northwest corner of the park and throwing cigarette butts everywhere. I told the other volunteers that I would go there and try to persuade them to put on shirts and pick up the butts. Then I went over and said politely, "Could you please put on your clothes? It doesn't look good when there are so many people around." One of them got angry, and shouted, "It's none of your business. I've been laid off. I can hardly afford to eat, and all you care about is stupid clothes." I was shocked at this rudeness. But I knew that he was upset, and could understand why he was nervous and unhappy. Yet I was also thinking, aren't we Chinese always saying that poverty should not deprive us of self-respect? Haven't we seen poor elderly people who wore old clothes and lived in harsh conditions, but were still fastidious about being clean? Is poverty any reason for uncivilized behavior? These thoughts flashed through my mind, and I had no idea what to say. I knew I was right, yet they defied me fiercely. It seemed as if I was the person doing something wrong. I was finally pulled away by other volunteers as the odds were against me.

I was greatly stimulated by this incident. I also figured out that the civilization of a society is directly related to economic development. The more powerful the country is, the richer the lives of its people are. Then they would pay greater attention to civilized manners.

Actually, most of the people I met during my volunteer work were quite reasonable. Only a few people snapped at me. Most of them were cooperative when I admonished them for spitting. They often said, "I'm sorry, I'll be careful next time," "Thank you for reminding me," "Sorry, I'll never let it happen again," "I feel so sorry, and I'll tell others to get rid of such a bad habit" or "We should change as the Olympics are approaching." I was greatly encouraged by their respect and understanding. It was only yesterday that I saw a middle-aged man in Financial Street spit as he walked to his car. I gave him a packet of tissue paper and a "civilization" card, urging him to show it to his acquaintances. He found a stain, crouched down to wipe it up, and said, "Thank you, I have to learn from you people. China would be a better place if everyone behaved like you. . . . " I saw him walk to a dustbin nearby, and throw the waste tissue in it. I was greatly moved at that time, and I believe that he will never spit in public again. The way he and other people react to our service is the best reward we could ask for.

I feel particularly warmed by the people we volunteers meet. Some of them are my friends now, and others have become outstanding anti-spitting volunteers. Besides, our organization is also supported by the Capital Civilization Office. The office has promised an unlimited supply of sputum tissue paper. We launched the "Holiday Civilized Action" by working together with the Beijing Municipal Bureau of Urban Management. Besides, the Beijing Municipal Health Administration has invited us to hold the "Healthy Olympics, Healthy Beijing" campaign to promote citizens' awareness of the importance of spitting in a civilized way. The administration has also provided us with some special tissue paper for sputum. Meanwhile, I have been encouraged by the leaders and colleagues in the company I work for. I can truly feel the changes in society and the ever-improving sense of social responsibility of our people. The changes can be partly attributed to my efforts, and I feel really happy about this. As a volunteer, this may be the biggest achievement for me. Besides, I am respected and recognized. I have found the value of my own life, experienced and witnessed the changing of the times, and seen our city become increasingly beautiful. Isn't this the greatest sense of achievement ever?

Now our Green Woodpecker organization has expanded its activities to Wenzhou, Chengdu and Changchun. Our activities are also available for all the Olympic cities, including Qingdao and Shenyang, although we need more volunteers. I will dedicate myself to this activity until there is no longer any uncivilized behavior in our cities.

*Is It Really That Difficult to Stop Spitting?*

It rained on the day I interviewed Wang Tao. Only a few foreign tourists were sitting in Starbucks Coffee, as it was Sunday morning. A middle-aged man in a bluish-grey suit sat at a table in the middle of the cafe, reading a thick press clipping album, with a computer bag and a large bulging recycling bag at his feet. I saw that his shoes were spotless—as if he had missed the rain. I recognized him as Wang Tao, as I had seen his photo on the volunteers' information website. He looked much maturer than I had expected.

If you didn't know the services offered by Wang Tao as a city cleaning volunteer in advance, it would be hard for you to imagine that such a gentleman could wipe up sputum with tissue paper in public. The dirty tissue paper may be kept in the big recycling bag he carries, when there is no dustbin nearby. And this dirt may be carried by him for a long distance. It's more difficult to imagine that such a gentle and modest person would give tissue paper to those who spit and throw cigarette butts, ask them to wipe or pick up the dirt, and remind them what they should do and what they should not do. Those people are not modest gentlemen like him.

Many people have expressed their appreciation and admiration for Wang Tao in newspaper articles. Yet Wang Tao, who sat in front of me, impressed me most with his simplicity. He told me honestly that from the very beginning to the real practice on the street, actually this process was a painful one. It required self-transcendence, similar to some kind of metamorphosis. He said that he attached great importance to the reports in the media, not for personal fame, but for some confirmation and encouragement from a mainstream group like the media, as he always hesitated and doubted, especially when he was misunderstood or in difficulties. Media encouragement helps him banish distracting thoughts and keep moving on.

Inside the recycling bag brought by Wang Tao were his tools and four kinds of tissue paper. These things well illustrated how he was recognized and supported by society. He bought the tissue paper at his own expense at the very beginning. Later the paper was supplied by the Capital Civilization Office, Beijing Municipal Bureau of Urban Management, Beijing Municipal Health Department and CYL Central Committee. These organizations provided him with free tissue paper carrying a printed code of conduct for civilized behavior. Wang Tao and his volunteer friends no longer need to buy such things themselves. Wang Tao, however, is still putting his own money into his volunteer work. He created the "China Anti-spitting Network" to promote relevant knowledge and civilized behavior with part of his family savings, and helps fund Green Woodpecker volunteer activities in other cities. The tissue paper is free, but not the postage. Wang Tao always has to pack and mail free tissue paper to branches of the Green Woodpecker organization in other provinces.

Among his treasures is a pair of white gloves. They are old and worn. According to Wang Tao, these gloves were used for self-protection while wiping up sputum. After all, sputum is also one source of communicable diseases. But he often barely had time to think about this, and he did the work without gloves many times. In addition, the Green Woodpecker organization can not provide each volunteer with a pair of gloves, so volunteers have to arrange personal protection themselves. To this end, Wang Tao hopes that some manufactures or sellers of disinfected wet paper towels can provide them with some of their products, even defective ones, to make the work of these woodpeckers safer and cleaner.

There are many stories about Wang Tao, and he writes diary on his blog every day. On the day I interviewed him, he had left home in Daxing at 6 a. m. Then he began his city cleaning volunteer work. He wiped up sputum and stains, curbed uncivilized behavior and picked up discarded garbage. He might carry the waste for a long distance until he finds a dustbin. The distance he walks does not take longer than that it takes others, but the time he spends is much more than that spent by others. If you see a man in a smart suit crouching down to remove sputum from the road, he may be Wang Tao or one of Wang's partners.

# Postscript

In the early summer of 2007, Ms. Zhang Hai'ou, Deputy Editor-in-Chief of the New World Press, brought me a research topic under the title of "The Dreams and Reality of Chinese Youth," telling me that the China International Publishing Group and her company intended to publish a book on this topic as one of the approaches to "getting the rest of the world to know about China." Through interviews with young Chinese people, covering their outlook on life, their thoughts, their dreams and their encounters with the world as it is, she said, "we will show the outside world China's reality, and the attitudes and viewpoints of China's younger generation."

This idea made me think of *The American Dream*, which was a worldwide sensation and won a Pulitzer Prize. Ms. Zhang and I found ourselves in total agreement, and set to work to plan how we were to choose interviewees to tell their real-life stories.

First, I posted a notice on my website "An Dun's Women's Website" and on my Sina blog. It was the first time for us to test the feasibility of this topic, and we were only too happy with the results. Almost every day we got e-mails from people wanting to be interviewed. I then set about interviewing and writing.

It was a very happy time for me, and I was frequently moved by the interviewees. I felt clearly the pulse of the time and the spirit of contemporary Chinese people in the stories of these strangers from different walks of life, having different living conditions and different cultural backgrounds. I could always sense their courage, honesty, magnanimity and wisdom in their sincere chats. Even when they expressed loneliness or regret—and their stories were not all sunny—I was still deeply touched, since it was what I had expected to find and was searching for: the simplicity and truth of life.

The interviewing process lasted a long time, and many people I interviewed are the most ordinary young people, whom you or I could meet in the street, striving to realize their dreams with their stories and thoughts. At this time I was often asked, "Why don't you choose famous and successful people since you intend to get the rest of the world to know about China? Aren't their intriguing stories more attractive, instructive and encouraging?" But I decided to record the life of ordinary people, since celebrities have many opportunities to tell their stories, while those who reached me only through the e-mail or a message on the Internet needed me to listen to them and write their stories down. Their struggles and trials, successes and failures, strike a chord in the hearts of ordinary people just like us. Since they are still struggling, and trying, and may still fail, we can learn from them, and draw courage and strength from their stories as we identify with them. They are like mirrors which enable us to see ourselves in them.

In 2008, the book was published as *The Chinese Dream*. Now it has become a series and a project rather than just one book. There will be more and more ordinary but touching stories of dream followers approaching us and sharing their feelings with us. Therefore, I will have more chances to contact the interviewees.

I have received many letters from readers since the book was published. Readers, moved and encouraged by the heroes of the book have expressed their hope of being interviewed by me. A student-turned-lecturer at an American university after years of study there wrote to me that "I have read here many books on the contemporary life of my Chinese compatriots as well as books on China for international readers. These books are all well written. But your book makes me feel different. While reading the life stories of those young people, I feel as if they were part of my life—my old neighbors and colleagues or even my family members. I am familiar with them and I understand them since I used to be one of them. I feel as if I myself have cherished their dreams, and experienced their frustrations, hesitations and struggles. Probably this is the strength of reality. What I find in this book is a real China full of vigor and hope. It is my hope that more international readers can learn about young Chinese people as well as China from this book since it gives an account of what my motherland and my compatriots really look like. I am 46 years old. Never did I think of telling the stories of the first half of my life until I read your book that presents a stage for us ordinary people. I would like to share my stories with you and your readers if you do not consider me out of date. In this way I can introduce China to the world along with others. " His letter gave me the most honest and sincere encouragement. Now he is one of my interviewees under the Project.

Apart from receiving encouragement from readers, the book was also awarded the prize of "CIPG's Excellent Foreign Publicity Book in 2008," and was acclaimed by international readers and publishers at the British and Frankfurt book fairs. The copyright of the book has been licensed in other countries as well. All these successes should be attributed to the brilliant, real-life stories of my interviewees. After all, there is nothing more touching than these stories.

I would like to express my sincere gratitude to all those who volunteered to be interviewed. Without you, this book would never have seen the light of day. I would also like to thank the editors of the China International Publishing Group and those of the New World Press for their trust in me and for giving me this opportunity to meet these ordinary but wonderful people. In addition, I owe a debt of gratitude to Mr. Zhao Qizheng, a pioneer in "getting the rest of the world to know about China," who managed to find time to write the foreword to this book. Special thanks also go to Mr. Yang Yuqian, President of the New World Press, and his colleagues Ms. Zhang Hai'ou and Ms. Li Shujuan for their selfless support and help, from which I benefited a lot. Meanwhile, I extend special gratitude to Lin Liangqi, former associate Editor-in-Chief of the China International Publishing Group. The original idea of "The Dreams and Reality of Chinese Youth" was thought up by this senior expert. Although I have had no chance to meet Mr. Lin yet, it is already a great honor for me to hear his valuable opinions and suggestions during my communication with the editor, which provided great help and improvement for my interview and writing.

Now my interviewees, as well as I myself, are to be examined by the readers. My greatest wish is that the readers can, just like me, learn something about the life from the stories of these ordinary people, and find the splendor of humanity and the beauty of life in the friends around them.

An Dun

*March* 20, 2009

图书在版编目(CIP)数据

　　一百个中国人的梦.2,当代百姓生活实录:英文/安顿著.
—北京:新世界出版社,2009.7
　　ISBN 978-7-5104-0407-8

　　Ⅰ.一… Ⅱ.安… Ⅲ.报告文学—作品集—中国—当代—英文　Ⅳ.1253.7
　　中国版本图书馆 CIP 数据核字(2009)第 104752 号

The Chinese Dream – Real-Life Stories of the Common People in Contemporary China
一百个中国人的梦(二):当代百姓生活实录

作　　　者:安　顿
插　　　图:李　钺
翻　　　译:同文世纪(李央　张瑞卿　潘大庆)
策　　　划:林良旗　张海鸥
责任编辑:李淑娟　葛文聪
英文审定:Paul White　徐明强
封面设计:青青虫工作室
版式设计:北京图腾视觉图文设计中心
责任印制:李一鸣　黄厚清
出版发行:新世界出版社
社　　　址:北京市西城区百万庄大街 24 号(100037)
总编室电话:+86 10 6899 5424　　　68326679(传真)
发行部电话:+86 10 6899 5968　　　68998705(传真)
本社中文网址:http://www.nwp.cn
本社英文网址:http://www.newworld-press.com
版权部电子信箱:frank@nwp.com.cn
版权部电话:+86 10 6899 6306
印刷:北京中印联印务有限公司
经销:新华书店
开本:787×1092　　　1/16
字数:170 千字　　印张:13.5
版次:2009 年 6 月第 1 版　2009 年 6 月北京第 1 次印刷
书号:ISBN 978-7-5104-0407-8
定价:48.00 元